BETTER OFF DEAD
10 FACTORS to consider before Calling it QUITS

Antoinette Randall

This is a nonfiction work. Certain names, locations, and characters are used fictitiously to protect their identities.

While the author has made every effort to provide accurate Internet addresses at the time of publication, neither the publisher nor the author assumes any responsibility for errors or for changes that occur after publication.

Dedication

To the burdened and distraught individuals who struggle with seeing life beyond misery, chaos, losses, and hurt. To those who desire to move forward, yet the darkness of gloom overtakes your drive. To those who continuously contemplate their existence.

"If you're open to giving yourself a chance, then I'm willing to challenge you to live!

In Memory of My Mother, Lady Priscilla Holmes, who slept away during the pre-order phase of this book. She did not take her life, but rather rendered it the benefit of humanity. She saw the printed proof of this book and I read a portion of Factor 5 to her on December 25, 2018.

I had no clue that it would be my final opportunity to: enjoy her energy, embrace her soft body, smell her hair, taste her food, feel her skin, admire her ever-changing nail polish, kiss her cheek, and gaze into her bluish-grey eyes.

She completed her Earthly assignment on January 8, 2019 and I put a fork in launching this book until I could conjure the strength to move forward.

For the most part, I was selfish and very angry, but I was reminded that her life wasn't all about me.

My Mother loved her creator and daily committed her life to serving his people, of all backgrounds, ages, gender and religious affiliations. She's outstandingly popular in the community and has indeed made her mark in history.

She taught me: how to read and comprehend, how to be a woman of prestige, how to handle business and keep records, how to care for my husband, how to respect people regardless of their status, how to serve without excuse, how to put my feelings aside for the higher purpose, and how to humble myself under the mighty hand of God. Her duty to me is fulfilled as she equipped me for life in priceless ways.

Although I still have intense moments of sadness, I am proud of what she consistently represented and further honored to even have existed in her world! Just as she was actively proud of me, I frequently expressed my admiration for how she gave 100% to her life. She has now been promoted to eternal freedom and happiness. The joy and perfection in her new world are incomparable to life on Earth, as we know it.

How could I possibly have an issue with that?
Even though a chunk of me left with her, I vow to
OWN this life of mine and show up with
competency, urgency and pride, as she instructed.

"We all have a job to do and only so much time to
do it. Let every man abide in his or her calling".

The Incredibly Unique and Irreplaceable,

Priscilla Holmes

Author's Truth

Because I study people and data, this book is credible. *Because I became a statistic,* well, that makes this book valid. I became that woman who totally lost sight of who I was, due to depression taking over my world. When I was expecting my first child, a family member instructed me to prepare myself for the terrible thoughts that come along after giving birth. If you would accept my unsparing honesty, I even judged this family member for admitting her truth that I couldn't fathom. In that moment of her transparency and my opinion, she became selfish and unfit to be a mother for revealing such things. She was talking about psychological and emotional issues that many are afraid or hesitant to acknowledge.

In certain cultures, weakness is characterized by displaying anything other than strength and power. Because I had yet to walk down the path that she spoke of, I silently rejected her notice.

When the time came, I gave birth to my first child, then quickly became pregnant with my second.

Needless to say, I hit postpartum depression full force, totally oblivious to the previous warning I was given. My daily routine along with the associated feelings allowed little to no room to acknowledge my very existence.

Seems like I was frustrated most of the time and was seldom happy with anything. For the next few years, I was in a sunken place, often wondering why my life was such a drag. My husband recognized the change and tried to uplift me, but I was too deep. He couldn't reach me nor did I stretch out my arms to be recovered. The kids gave me a sense of joy, but there was a barrier that prevented me from fully enjoying motherhood like I do now.

While I never contemplated suicide during that time, I did question my reason for existing; especially, when I totally lost the vision for my life. No, it wasn't for a moment in time. It started as days and developed into years of my life that I will never be able to reclaim. Learning how to defeat depression is one of my greatest victories. Since breaking free, I've never craved running back into its invisibly-uncomforting arms.

Depression will ruin relationships and destroy opportunities. It will cause you to exist as the walking dead. I have come to understand that we can save ourselves a heap of trouble, if we stop rejecting wisdom and adhere to wise counseling. The issue is, we unreasonably expect messengers to be perfect; therefore, we miss the opportunity to get the breakthrough so desperately needed. My purpose for writing this piece is to connect with those who suffer with mild to severe depression by revealing the reality of several factors that spark and cultivate this spirit of gloom. I consider it a need for me to tackle this subject, bring awareness, and free as many minds as possible.

This book is a reference to the causes of depression, its symptoms, human behavior, and healthy tips for those sincerely desiring to overcome depression and suicidal imaginations. I chose to keep it honest, without any sugar, as *"accepting the reflection in the mirror"* is one of the best prerequisites to making a change. Your mind can indeed be set free from the life-altering shackles, that come for one purpose: to turn you into a victim of purpose suicide, one negative thought at a time!

The day has arrived for you to come out of withdrawal, to turn the lights and music back on, to open the curtains, to unrhythmically dance in the rain, and to lift your head above the dirty water. It's time to live my love. Depression can take control and disfigure your perspective, but as the owner of your mind, **you have the authority** to evict it from the premise of your soul and experience *mind-liberation*. May the words in this piece cause you to rise from the defeat of sorrow and into the zone of hope, because you're not alive to contemplate death, but to LIVE!

Introduction

People tend to express clueless shock when informed of a death by way of suicide. When the cause of death is revealed as an apparent suicide, eyes stretch and hands go over mouths right before the questions and comments began.

"I had no idea that they were struggling with anything", seems to be the most popular response. A huge fib exists. It says you have to be along the lines of unemployment, financial shambles, or a struggling single mother in order to experience mental and emotional chaos. LIES. You may be under the assumption that it only affects certain people and you'd know if someone were suffering with depression or suicidal thoughts.

Just as a snake can sneakily spy on you from the grass while you're unsuspecting, so can an individual fake their feelings of happiness and contentment. Some of the very people whose lives you'd love to have, whom you consider "powerful", are silently suffering; numbering their days, believing death is far more peaceful than life. Depression and suicide are more than the typical well-known acts. There are various forms of depression, that you are probably battling right now, totally unaware of its presence.

Fantastic news! You don't have to live in a dark tunnel for the rest of your life. There are various ways and sources available for those who are suffering. While psychotherapy (talk therapy) is one effective way to assist those in a crisis, many are skeptical about "letting it all out" to a stranger. Then you have those who are willing; however, their financial status doesn't allow room to compensate a counselor or psychiatrist. Others groups of people are in denial regarding depression and wouldn't dare go to a shrink to be labeled as a lunatic. Although that is not always the case, it's their stance.

One thing about a book is, you don't need an appointment to read it. Once it's in your possession, it can always be accessed and referenced at any time.

My wish is for this particular book to bring clarity, understanding, and a solution to those willing to give it a chance. *Although it is undeniably convincing, it is not claimed as the final answer or top solution for ending depression and suicidal compulsions.* Even a certified mental health expert is unable to prevent such things; however, if an individual is ready to commit to the recommended practices and procedures regarding the state of their lives, with optimism, they can successfully rise from the darkness of both. You have to be willing to put in the work for your own tranquility, whether a professional is involved or not.

All people experience problems, some more horrendous than others. One thing for sure, if problems aren't properly managed, they will diminish the mind to dark areas of hopelessness.

I don't know what may have occurred in your life, but I'd like to offer you the chance to see what you consider "the end" as an incredible opportunity to start fresh. This read will coach you regarding the elimination of factors that lead to your demise and those that should be adapted to pull you from the dungeon, into optimism.

When people want to give up, they don't need a 6 o'clock pity-party. They need reasons to live again, love again or to believe in themselves for the first time.

That's it. People need reasons to TRY again. May this read assist you with realizing the reasons why you must *Try* to thrive, with maximum measure, because you're better off *Alive!*

Factor 1

Under the Microscope. Understanding is the Beginning of Getting Better

In order to know how to properly manage, heal, or rise from the darkness of depression, you must understand and be honest about where you stand mentally.

There are various forms of depression, with the most extreme leading to suicide.

When you sit with a therapist, questions are asked regarding your feelings, regrets, goals, etc.

Knowing key details about your thought process

will greatly assist with the style of treatment you undergo. Pride has to be denied and the mind has to be open. When you want to LIVE, toss all imaginations about being judged out of the window. It's about putting all of the cards on the table in order to locate the root of the depression, which aids in determining the applicable measures.

A person doesn't decide to stop living, out of the clear blue, but this option is selected after arriving to the point of no longer having the willingness to deal. *The key is to reach people before they arrive to that point!* Below I have listed and combined familiar terms to further explain how they appear in the lives of humans. Of course, I've added a twist and will present the terms from various angles for descriptive and analytic reasoning. Looking at these uniquely described terms will also show that more people are closer to the edge than they realize.

Suicide *is more than the typical well-known acts.* It is a spirit of despair that will drive out every ounce of hope until the individual is deemed lifeless. It is not an immediate decision, but there are levels to actually getting to the point of going through with the indefinite act.

Information in this book will focus on the *following* aspect of suicide; as it's the gateway to the former.

Purpose Suicide occurs when people decide to stop giving a crap about themselves, when they totally lose interest in giving certain portions of life a fighting chance. They may appear as a success *from the surface level*, but beneath lies feelings of inadequacy and sorrow. If you are prevented from rendering what you love to life, it will make you feel as though you're imprisoned.

You get to this place by handcuffing yourself. Limitations such as: fears, barriers, worries, and the opinions of people, will taint your possibilities, kill your drive, and destroy your chances. You might even slap your own head, wondering *"what in the world is wrong with me"*, but it's frequently the unseen forces that causes your mental detour. You are alive for a great reason. Anything or person who wishes to persuade or manipulate you astray from productive significance is leading you to the slaughter house. While they are too coward to take your life, your obedience to them will land you between a rock and wall of steel.

When blocks are respected more than purpose, you are shackling yourself. When you attend to everything except those matters concerning your purpose, you will be just as exhausted as a man pulling a truck from the ditch, by his own strength. After so many unsuccessful attempts, you won't be interested in too much outside of contemplating your existence. **This is purpose suicide**. Roadblocks along the path are misunderstood. So many people respect blocks to the point of quitting altogether. Afterall, a block is an indication of trouble or construction ahead, right? Wrong. Happiness could very well be beyond the blocks seen!

You are only fought by opposition, because *something within you is feared* by outside forces.

You are only stopped, because your moving ahead means that others will have a chance to lift their heads above water.

It means that you are one less person to honor the faulty idea that you're better off dead.

Deciding to quit gives victory to that invisible demon, sent to deter you from thriving. This is one reason why you are fought more when trying to excel.

Anyone sitting still only poses a threat to one person; themselves. There is no victory over depression when sitting within the cycle of it. If anything, idleness puts you in the perfect position to ponder depressive notions.

In terms of roadblocks, have you ever wondered what your life might look like if you actually mapped out traveling a different way or moving the barrier that blocks your path? What may appear as a reason to stop could be a reason to accelerate. Giving up, changing your mind, or putting it off for later are all versions of *Purpose Suicide*.

✓ Key Note: Temporary and short-lived spouts of sadness does not qualify as depression, so it would be unnecessary to categorize yourself in any of the following categories.

Keeping your personal affairs private for the sake of sacredness is one thing, but putting up a facade in attempt to fool others; thereby, keeping them from asking questions is a form of **Suppressive-Depression.** People in this category will go to engagements, host events, and surprisingly be the life of the party. Their high is temporary, ran off just enough false energy to totally redirect everyone's attention away from their unfortunate truth. These people will not linger around bliss for too long, because it is in direct conflict with their spirit of gloom. In the act of suppression, an individual is conscious (well aware) of what they're doing. Caught off guard, their countenance may reveal their negative internal feelings. They may also zone out or their personality will alter.

Suppression is like opening yourself up for love repeatedly, without ridding yourself of the debris from previous relationships.

It's like stacking living bodies on top of each other and kind of hoping that those people will keep quiet until they eventually die.

Sounds gruesome; however, this is what people are doing to themselves when they carry on in this fashion. Antidepressants are prescribed for this type of depression, but please note that the effect of these pills are not in support of eradicating deep pain and healing you emotionally. They are suppressants, which are supposed to alleviate the symptoms; however, they fall quite short of that claim. This is not my opinion, but based off facts that are supported by real life testimonials, statistics, and research.

A person who professionally operates in suppression could unquestionably fool people. Foremost, it takes a spiritually attuned or discerning person to pick up on depressive-suicidal vibes. Next, people who don't want anyone in are masters in terms of existing within illusions. This is how you could be out celebrating with an associate, then find out the very next day that they ended their life. If you aren't in tune and they aren't willing to *let you in*, the chance to help them expires. Look out for the following statements:

"Don't worry about me. I'm better than ever."

"Everything is great."

"I'm not the one with the problem, it's you."

It's one thing to speak in optimism and another to lie. Being optimistic is knowing your reality, yet living beyond what the eyes can see. Speaking by Faith is awesome; moreover, you have to live according to what you claim to believe. This is the problem with suppression. It sweeps the foul-smelling debris under the rug and lights candles in attempt to disguise the hidden odor.

If you say you're better than ever, it would be a contradiction to drown in your troubles once everyone is outside of your presence. If you believe that everything will work out, it would be inconsistent to stress and go on tirades about your issues. The mind must be trained to believe that obstacles can't keep you away from better days. Regardless of the destruction that has swept rampantly through your world, you can still witness better, if you're willing to live to see it happen.

1.1 Suppression gone bad.

If a person has a history of being mocked and criticized for something, they may shy away from it in the future. Given the chance to engage in the matter again, the exact feelings that were evident in the past will flood the individual, just as if they were reliving that moment. Some people will have a full-blown anxiety attack.

Bottling up emotions, telling yourself that you will get over through the course of time, is a bad idea. It will spew out during inopportune times and in awkward ways. The person may actually get to the point to where they can't stomach themselves, due to the ugly transformation that suppression has brought to their lives. Some will dispute this data-rich fact by suggesting that their ability to remain emotionless is a form of utilizing self-control. The source of the problem may not suffer the explosion of your emotions, but your health will. You can't bottle up chaos and expect for it to remain intact. There is a war inside that's fighting to burst through.

Surprise is the reaction of seeing the strongest member of the family lying in a hospital bed, due to breakdown, heart attack, or stroke, but a chunk of these issues have been ushered in by the close relative of suppression; **repression**, which is a form of archiving that lives deep within the level of your mind that no one knows about except you. After continually forcing certain things to the back of your memory, due to the emotions that it sparks, that you clearly are opposed to dealing with, you enter into **Repressive-Depression.**

If a child is constantly rebuked for *allegedly* talking too much or asking dumb questions, they may develop into an adult who gives minimal to no effort towards effective communication. As an adult, they may never acknowledge or account their lack of communication to the repeated scorn received as a child.

✓ Key Point

In fully matured repression, the person is not aware of the underlying reason for why they think and respond the way that they do. Because of their routine of tossing pain over their shoulder for so long, they will not recognize or acknowledge the culprit behind their character flaws. They have squashed the memory to the point of it becoming vague.

I am compelled to briefly discuss repression from the spectrum of recovery. If I could give it a term, I'd call it **psy-gression** (mentally processing and the pondering of required or necessary imaginations, plans, and memories) and define it as the ability to recall details as if it just occurred; however, discussing it is a long shot. It may even go to the grave undisclosed. In their own way, the person makes peace with the situation and deems it unnecessary to further reference, as the mentioning of it serves no dire purpose.

Reminiscing is avoided because it can cause one to regress to emotions that disrupt current peace and harmony.

Some will argue that a person exercising in psygression is not over that particular memory, because they opt out of talking about it, yet when they think about it, emotions rise up. In psygression, people can carry on even though they have been screwed over time and time again. They are aware of what they've come through;

furthermore, they have come to terms with yesterday. Yes, they have emotions, but are not governed by them. Although they don't condone the past, they refuse to allow it to control their lives by submitting to any state of mind that ultimately leads to their demise.

The **Miserably Depressed** are immensely difficult to deal with. As they live in misery, they will ensure that everyone in their immediate space suffers the consequence of their wrath. When these individuals speak, they are careless with their words and the style by which they speak. They say things like,

"This is the way that I've always been and I refuse to change!"

"If you can't accept me, you can hit the door!"

"If I were you, I wouldn't get married to that woman/man. They remind me of the pig that ruined my life!"

"College is a waste of time and no job will pay you enough to cover all of that debt you've accumulated. You're better off getting a job like everyone else, while you're guaranteed one."

They are not happy with anything that anyone can do or say to them. They will find a reason to complain; for example, if you take them out for a nice meal, instead of them showing gratitude, they may slam your effort and announce their disgust for the food, traffic on the road, temperature outside, or even the flavor of gum you're chewing. These people are like rust-colored water, that begins dripping through the ceiling, as soon as you get new carpet. It could be that they were frequently rejected by someone they trusted, a string of negative occurrences that completely destroyed their buoyancy, or one large and nasty heartbreak that landed them in this dispirited position.

Miserably depressed people will slice your good intentions in half. They will have the firmest people crying and turn organization into chaos.

Positive vibes will quickly dissipate when a person of this spirit enters a room.

After living as miserably depressed for so long, the person becomes complacent and could care less as to how they come off to others. In plenty cases, they are actually unaware of their depression. They figure that their actions are fine and it's everyone else that's insane. I call this **Miserably Repressed-Depression.**

Matters that should be kept private and those that should be shared has caused much debate over the years, but we should all be clear on this: if you are having trouble focusing on your future, dealing with negative emotions and can't figure out the cause, or imagining heinous acts against yourself or others, you need to talk to someone!

The human mind is like a computer. Files featured on the home screen and those that are archived are totally at the discretion of the owner. Allowing too much tainted information to crowd the computer system, could lead to getting a virus. In extreme cases, the computer will crash. Now, what about the human mind?

How much pain and anguish can it revisit over and over again without *freezing*?

When the mind is overwhelmed and unable to refresh, the person views suicide as the doorway to *shutting down*! Constantly bringing up situations and wallowing in the pain, without ever getting aid is torment on the mind and an enemy to the soul. For this reason, help is necessary and I urge you to be proactive about saving your mind, your life.

Depression is real folks and there are many causes and forms. If it is not properly managed, it will pollute the purpose for living and in fully developed cases, suicide. Many are in denial and labeling depression as something else. Others are totally unaware of this destructive spirit and believe that what they are experiencing is a healthy commonality of the human experience.

- If it takes counseling, go and empty your thoughts. They are trained to handle it.
- If it takes prayer, say everything that you're ashamed to say to people. Get relief.
- If it takes a mentor, accept the truth and move forward in confidence.
- If it takes a support group, ponder the advice. They have traveled that road.
- If it takes self-acclamation, that's feasible as well; however, it takes accountability and

commitment. If you are one who procrastinates, this is not the best option.

<u>Factor 1 Challenge</u>

Now, we know that everyone is not ready to meet with a psychotherapist or psychiatrist, as discovered back in the late 19th century with Sigmund Freud, the founder of psychoanalysis, however, sometimes it must be escalated to that level.

This is why it's essential to be honest about yourself and know what you're dealing with in terms of depression.

People hear the root word *psycho* and automatically associate it with being a maniac, but please don't jump on the boat of believing you're a psychopath. Seeking out help proves that you are wise and well aware of your right to care about yourself others.

Factor 2

Money is Not Always the Solution

As long as you have money, you will have a great life, right? LIES. Money can indeed be improperly regarded.

For centuries, money has been used in attempt to measure the status of humans, as a method of coping, and as refuge; however, it repeatedly falls short of the purpose it's misrepresented to accomplish. Money has a standard use, yet society has placed it on the highest peak as the god that all humans should worship, but when life inevitably plummets, people are left in an unforeseen state, because money, if nothing else, was professed as the panacea for all issues.

There is a general purpose for cash and coins, to exchange and purchase goods and services. It is also used to determine the overall worth of an individual. If you research your favorite celebrity, the results may also inform you of their worth, which is based off the value of their money and possessions.

The deluded view of money has set families at odds, divided cultures of people, ruined marriages, tainted self-worth views, and one of the leading causes of people feeling as if they can't accelerate in life; especially when in lack of this resource.

When you have never kissed riches, your thoughts may be similar to, "If I were rich, I wouldn't have a care in the world. I'd have everything that I need." The trouble with that statement is, it's much more to that belief system. It's simple to say what you would do if you were in a definite position; distinctly if you have yet to walk through it.

When an individual is constantly broke (financially deficient), they presume that money will tackle all of their problems. Wealth may grant you a seat at the table of prominent figures, but it will not revoke your membership from the depression club. If wealth were the answer to fulfillment, the financially elite would be free from battling with depression, inadequacy, and suicidal behavior. Money is not the solution when the issue is beyond socioeconomic status.

From their virgin perspective, it's insane for a rich person to be grief-stricken, friendless and in despair. After all, the wealthy can buy anything right?

Wrong.

- Money will allow you to rent out a party space for the night, but it can't guarantee you a loyal friend during seasons of drought.

- Money can take you to breathtaking islands, but it can't guarantee you a stress-free experience, considering everything that has to be tackled once you're back to reality.

- Money can even buy you an exceptional attorney, but it can't clean up your reputation.

The abundance of money can make life more convenient, but it's inefficient with handling issues that are resistant to money.

Money is powerful, yet friendship, health and love is not available for purchase in stores or online.

Money and materials can make life quite convenient, but if your mind is so damaged beyond healthy function, what's the benefit of money or the materials?

That's kind of like becoming a millionaire at the expense of losing body extremities from an auto accident. You can indeed pay people to assist you in your daily routine, but you'll never have the freedom to do it yourself. In addition, without the presence of money, your support system will be reduced by a substantial percent.

A good job or lucrative career may get you the materials and possessions that you've always wanted, but eventually you will wonder why the feelings of emptiness and defeat continue. You are a human who has needs that money can't appease. Money is powerless in terms of emotional and spiritual needs. As humans, there are certain things that are pertinent to our survival. When the sense of belonging is under attack, some feel as though they have no reason to live.

When you don't feel empowered or relevant in your routine dealings, you may find yourself dispirited and in search for what makes you feel alive.

As humans, we must see life on a larger scale, not just from the aspect of money. Of course, it's quite an essential resource to have; however, basing total happiness off how much you're worth, according to the standards of society is unreasonable. So many measure themselves according to what's popular in the media, which is a false perception of truth.

Advantages and Barriers of Money:

The abundance of money can make some feel untouchable, yet they are bound to the needs that come along with being human.

Money can buy a date, but does not promise intimacy.
Money can land you the deed to a breathtaking estate, yet a home isn't guaranteed.
Money can buy a cosmetic procedure, but offers no relief for internal feelings of ugliness.
Money can purchase an alcoholic beverage, but it will never eliminate the alleged need for a drink.
Money can grant a night of sex, but it does not guarantee a love making session.
Money can buy flowers, but it does not right previous wrongs.
Money can buy a tank of gas, but there is no promise to get you anywhere far.
Money can buy a Hollywood smile, but joy is not inclusive with the new set of teeth.
Money can hire a personal committee, but the prevention of backstabbing and blackmail does not come in the contract.

Money can purchase clothing, but it does not tweak your unadulterated opinion of yourself.
Money can hire the best attorney, but it does not mean you will avoid incarceration.
Money can buy antidepressants; however, it will not deal with the root of depression.
Money can buy you a Valentine and boat ride, but it will never repair a broken heart.
Money can afford you a fairy-tale wedding, but true untainted love, well, that will always be something that money will never be able to compete with.

If you have experienced any of the aforementioned, you can certainly attest that money isn't as powerful as it's glorified to be.

The way that your heart feels is important and an abundance of money can't change that. What can money do if your best friend is on life support? What good is money if you-yourself have been given an expiration date? What good is money when you only desire to receive unconditional love?

Dear Reader, please put money in its proper place in your life. Don't give it an undeserved platform. Don't put it above those that you care for, because if you lose them, the money will fail to comfort you. Money is to be used to purchase the necessities we need and to enjoy life.

Don't use it to power over others. Don't use it to cover your lies and cheating antics. It will come back to bite you in your butt.

Remember that you are valuable, whether you're worth millions or even if you're standing in line for government assistance. Everything that you can see is temporary. Don't allow the absence of money to cause you to go under the ground. As long as you're breathing with the freedom to make decisions, money can be made.

Money is essential, but it is not god. Sometimes your name is enough to get you complimentary services, an endorsement, or a home that you paid nothing for. Perhaps you have never known anyone in your network to benefit in such a way, but trust me, it happens. Please understand that true worth far exceeds money.

Sitting around feeling sad because of financial loss, deficiency, or debt should not happen. It has no right to power over you in such a way unless you give it permission. In these times, there are so many ways to recuperate from monetary deprivation. Cease from the pity and get busy looking for ways to turn the page.

Factor 2 Challenge

This challenge is more so about understanding the influence of money on your current life and view of yourself.

1. Have you ever been in lack of money and totally lost the will to thrive?
2. Would the people in your network continue to linger around if your income were substantially less?
3. Would an absence of money get you dismissed from certain societies and groups?

Answers that reveal a totally different life and set of associates solely based off financial status, should be a compelling indication of the power that money has on your life. In addition to counting your cash, take some time to sum up the reasons why you are valuable to society or your immediate surroundings. When you have nothing to offer except money, you have lost sight of what living is all about.

Factor 3

Clean Up Your Circle

Your choice in associates can weigh heavy on your opinion about yourself. Often times, people tend to respect the perspectives of their closest friends, even if they are negative. This can lead you down a dark road of feeling alone even though you're in the presence of alleged, friends. The way you feel is a great indication as to what is. You frequently sense that you are alone, because *you are*. While an unbiased perspective is a bonus to have, some associates happen to be that piece of hair that ruins your entree and appetite!

If you've been feeling like an outcast, although you have friends, please consider the following.

A TRUE FRIEND:

- sees beyond the facades used in attempt to hide actual feelings.
- knows when their pal isn't in the mood to talk or go out.
- is honest and upfront concerning issues that their buddy is associated with.
- wouldn't observe their associate having repeated off-days without inquiring.
- wouldn't stand by and watch their friend make a fool of themselves.
- will defend their counterpart during the most inopportune times.
- will show up for their best buddy, even when it's inconvenient.

Do you have people around who are aware of your struggles and actively support you in the fight to overcome?

Now, although I'm asking you these questions, please note that friendship is not one-sided. If you expect support and loyalty from your friends, you should be quick to demonstrate the same. If you are private concerning your affairs in life, then you would need to respect the privacy of your friends. Respect their wishes and appreciate their differences.

It's important to know your circle.

Friends don't have to call or text daily; nonetheless, they should know that they can count on each other. Care is shown at any chance it's given. Disagreements will occur, but true friends can make it past difficult times. If you wrong your friend, apologize with them and make peace.

Bodily waste in the toilet will start to stink up the bathroom if the toilet is never flushed.

Don't allow the funk to linger.

Make the offense known through a discussion and clear the air. This will eliminate the weird and uneasy feeling that accompanies seeing them later on in passing. Never blow it off as, "it'll pass in time". You may stop thinking about it, but something is sure to occur that will refresh your memory and you'd much rather had made peace, as opposed to handling it within the silence of your own mind. No one else may ever know how you feel, but you do.

Speaking of no one else being aware, sometimes friends may not know that you were hurt by something. Sweeping it under the rug gives permission for it to continue. Repeated offenses are symbolic that you need to cut ties, because they could obviously care less about the way that you feel.

Keeping people in your life that habitually hurt you will weigh on you in ways unimaginable.

If a friend decides that they no longer want to deal with you, due to a disagreement, then go with that. It may cause some friction and hurt, but at least it gives closure.

Friends should be open and honest with each other. If you are constantly kept in the dark, ignored and uninformed regarding the matters of a friend, that's a questionable and lonely place to be in.

If you are announced as a friend, that should automatically remove you from the stranger list.

When people make it known that they are better off without you, accept it. You don't have to beg anyone to see your true value.

Everyone isn't seeking a loyal friend, although they claim to. They are so adapted to others straddling the fence with them, that it's the only version of a friend that they're familiar with. You could attempt to be the only light along their path; nonetheless, don't forget to calculate what it's costing you.

If you are putting out positive energy concerning friendship, don't worry if it's not reciprocated. It's only a matter of time before the atmosphere shifts in your favor. Dry your tears and cease from questioning your worth in terms of friendship. There are billions of people in this world and it's unreasonable to get depressed over a few that aren't receptive to or deserving of a friend like you.

1.1 Bad for Business. Blockers of Pleasure

Not sure if you know this, but some friends are bad for business and pleasure. Associating yourself with certain individuals can cause substantial damage to your life. If their character is tasteless, yours will be questioned, due to association.

Believe it or not, some people have even been disregarded for ideal positions, due to certain people that they're adamant about keeping around. Potential courtships have passed the "unaware" because of their opinionated and bitter buddies that stand as barriers, preventing anything from getting serious.

Associates that always have a complaint or sour opinion about everything can cause you to literally lose your appetite and excitement for life. It would be in your best interest to leave them behind when their company continuously causes negative friction in your world. Just as your choice in a spouse can redirect or off-center your life, so can your selection of friends.

Make it a point to familiarize yourself with their character. In retrospect, have they earned the right to remain in your world?

While it's true that everyone is unique, you don't want their differences to stain your reputation or run off others that genuinely care for you. One of the aims of a staff meeting is to reveal information in order to ensure that everyone is on the same page. This also applies to friendship. Now, I don't expect anyone to arrange a sit-down with written contracts for their friend to sign. I'm sure that some would find that a bit awkward.

It's essential to know those in your camp. Take notice of the way that they speak and the words chosen to get their point across. Keep your eyes open concerning their character overall.

Observe the way that they handle their family members and associates. How do they value the lives of others, material possessions, and their vocational position? If they have a poor attitude towards their own life, what chance is there that they will value yours? If they have a habit of trash talking others, it's only a matter of time before they verbally throw you under the bus.

Far in the distant moonlight, a dog and a fox may resemble each other. Make no mistake about it, they are two different animals with opposing needs. If they are seen together, a fight just ended or it's about to begin. As humans grow from infant stage into adulthood, they should constantly undergo changes; however, not everyone evolves. Some change for the worse, others for the best, and then there are those who believe that remaining the same, keeps them loyal to the village that raised them.

If you ran into an old schoolmate and noticed that they were still carrying on as they did in elementary school, you'd probably wonder about the freeze within their level of maturity. At some point in time, life should prompt humans to make changes. If you're someone who values life along with your decisions, your friends should have the same or better values. It's such an advantage to be in a network of individuals who can introduce you to undiscovered paths and challenge you to new horizons.

Many of you are dragging dead-weight friends along. For that very reason, you haven't been able to make it too far. Your version of doing good may be the continuous act of working towards your goals. Their idea of doing good may involve living under the showering benefits of a cake daddy or sugar momma.

They will find a reason to complain or bring up all the reasons why you shouldn't attempt anything that will build your optimism for the future. You fear telling them of your latest thoughts, as you know doubtful and critical comments will follow. If you think that type of negativity is of no harm to you, you're wrong. For as long as you listen to it, without rebuke, it will eventually sink in. You will resort back to doing what makes them comfortable, which makes you miserable. You may never say it, but the stress of it on your mind and body will start to show.

If your alleged friends are not quick to celebrate or support you in making your life better, you are better off without them.

Individuals that you choose to listen to and confide in weigh heavily on your life, so make sure that they share common values with you. The good girl can only hang out with the bad boy for so long until she submits herself under his practices. Even if she never lives out everything as he, her silence concerning his wayward living shows that she condones it. Her commitment to him denounces her good morals, which points her allegiance to the bad boy culture. Yes, there's a chance that good can outshine bad; however, the weakest link will often succumb to the greater force. Some say, "My silence doesn't mean I support it".

While I can agree to a certain extent, the actions of a person will speak volumes. If you disagree with something, yet continue lingering around it in silence, your words become void.

When associates fail to compliment your life, go with it. It's not a good feeling to grow apart from those you undisputedly care for, but when they discharge more damage than good, the ties must be severed.

You wouldn't dare go into an interview wearing a shirt 4 sizes too small. Not only will the shirt command attention, but also taint your shot. It's time to face the truth. Like a too-small shirt, you have outgrown certain friends and keeping them around will negatively impact you in some form.

If for some reason you still feel obligated to give people a chance when their behavior has proved that they could care less about their reputation or yours, you have decided to inhibit yourself. Is that friend really worth the damage that they cause?

1.2 LOVE is Evident

Few people are loners, which leads to many running into the arms of "whomever is willing to give the attention desired".

Just in case you didn't know, a high cost is associated with dealing with self-serving individuals. They will suck you dry as a raisin, vanish from your life and leave you lifeless for the vultures to finish you off!

Being used and trashed like this leads to depression and in extreme cases, suicide.

Love is so important and some will sacrifice anything for a hint of it. But that's the kicker, with love, it's either real or fantasy. This is a short post from a blog of mine.

Love is patient and unconditional. Lust sees no benefit in waiting, because it's selfish. Lust isn't here today and gone tomorrow. Lust will leave you with a mess to clean up; By Yourself. Love doesn't have to be questioned. Lust will have you wondering about your relationship status. Don't allow your unreasonable 'list of wants' to keep you from being loved. Don't ignore the red flags of Lust just for the sake of 'having someone'. So many are stuck with feelings for people who only wanted a lustful 'test drive'.

When a matter has all of the signs of being cow manure, why would it need further evaluation when you're present for the visual and odor? *Even the flies show up as an indication.* Same rule applies to love. If you have to question it or falsify information to butter it up, it's more than likely eligible for the waste department.

What is it within you that makes you want to trust a snake with your heart and emotions?

Once a person reveals who they are, why add a comma?

There are many signs, if you care to pay attention. This is the factor: when people get what they've always wanted or never had, they're more willing to ignore the dark characteristics of their new beau. The quality attention, gift giving and ear whispering may be blissful in the beginning stage of a relationship, but over the course of time, it will wear off and those ugly areas will become more evident. I am not bashing love, but the deceitful imitation of it.

When you allow someone into your personal space, they will grow on you.

Many claim to have so much control, but when they are dumped or tricked, the emotions of hurt surface. If you were simply "hanging out or having fun", why would you feel angry, sad or disappointed when their actions display that you are not worth committing to?

It's because you are a human with feelings and emotions that mature, sometimes for the wrong people. While no courtship is perfect, the best interest for the other should always be top priority. When selfish decisions are made only for the interest of one, then the unconsidered person is better off alone. A unit is comprised of two or more.

Actions that show, "my way or the highway" is not a partnership. That's dictatorship that will eventually lead the slaughter house.

Love is serious and with so many being in line for a shot, the predators are also searching for who they can exploit.

There are steps and signs regarding love. It's nothing that should be entered into hastily. Rushing and forcing someone to love you will not only keep you single, but bleeding. Love is like a flower. Over the course of time, it will grow and flourish.

You have to know your worth and what you deserve. You also have to appraise the sacrifice for settling with a piece of someone's heart.

A broken heart is one of the worst things that a human can have.

It will cause people to withdraw to a lonely dark room. It will cause weight loss or weight increase. Some will put on a facade at work, then break down once in the privacy of their homes.

Some will began using conventional soothers as they struggle through the grieving process of a broken heart. Others will turn to promiscuity as a form of dealing. A number of people will totally denounce that love exists, due to their horrific experience of managing their grieving heart.

To me, love is worth the chance. Love, where both parties are unconditionally invested is worth the chance. If all factors point in the direction of love, then by all means give it a chance; but, if you KNOW that something's off, pass on the opportunity for future regret.

Yes, every relationship has problems, but those are called growing pains that both units are willing to smooth out together. If you're constantly left to clean a mess on aisle 3 that was collectively created, then you are alone.

- A thoughtful partner wouldn't allow their sweetheart to carry pressure alone.

- A thoughtful partner wouldn't see their spouse grieved and ignore them.

- A thoughtful partner wouldn't purposefully set out to harm their mate.

- A thoughtful partner wouldn't have sex with you, only to please themselves.

- A thoughtful partner wouldn't go out and spend money lavishly knowing the plans that are in place.
- A thoughtful partner wouldn't choose others over their lover.

A person who is with you for love may in fact become familiar with you, but they will remain committed to developing the relationship. Even in hard times, and they are many, your devotion for the vows should remain in effect. You may get mad at them, but their value in your eyes, should never fade.

Sure, go to another room to cool off if that will keep you from saying or doing something that you'll later regret. If they make a mistake, don't say, "I told you so". The consequence from the mistake is enough pressure.

Men are awesome beings; however, they can appreciate a woman who honors, respects and validates them for the men that they are.

Women are awesome beings; however, it's an incredible bonus when she has the allegiance, attention and admiration from her man, in all areas, not just physical.

If you found yourself getting emotional because you've never experienced love as I have described, it's okay. You're still alive, which indicates that you still have a shot at being loved.

Don't roll over and die, because some sucker is unaware of what true love is. Help yourself by ridding your zone of any person who isn't willing to commit to valuing your life.

This is about sustaining your life, not crippling it. I have heard so many excuses as to why people avoid marriage; however, if someone's good enough to do *everything* with except make vows, they just may be a selfish parasite.

While I respect that marriage isn't for everyone, it's terrible to be pro-single, yet date someone who strongly desires marriage. For those of you desiring a partnership from those who shun marriage, cease from giving these types of people the option to guess about whether or not they want to love you.

Factor 3 Challenge

Reconsider those who are closest to you. It's your right to decide who and what is suitable for your world. Make it your top priority to evaluate your circle and *clean it up*.

Factor 4

"...but I'm Lonely!"

Marriage is presumed as the answer to a host of things, including loneliness. No Ma'am. No Sir. Loneliness is not a singles' issue. You don't have to be a loner in order to be dominated by this irritant. Loneliness can actually be present in the life of someone who has a host of friends, family and associates. Vulnerability for deception is one of the main requirements that welcomes this force. It is a spirit of solitude that leads to the lower end of sorrow. This spirit deceives people into believing that they are undeniably alone in their world. It is indeed a gateway to depression and the cause for thousands to enter into commitments and relationships without any genuine thrill. They just don't want to be alone. Loss, identity crisis, boredom, and living without a beau are just a few reasons why people find themselves in the land of loneliness.

1.1 Loss

Losing anything of profound value can not only cause anger, but loneliness. Some things have more influence on our lives than others; for instance, losing a vehicle is not on the same level as losing a body extremity. Vehicles come a dime a dozen. They can be replaced. Prosthetics are made for individuals seeking mobility again; moreover, it will never be like the original.

Being terminated from a job that you gave your best performance on is another loss that causes discouragement, inadequacy, depression and loneliness.

When life releases darts (loss), we are sometimes burned, pained and scarred.

Now **death** can shake your world unlike anything else. Walking through the many stages of grief related to the **death** of a loved one is definitely a lonely and frustrating process. This is not about some distant relative or friend who passed, in which you feel nothing for. This is about losing someone who you shared a unique, personal and close connection with.

This is about your world being ripped in half. This is about attempting to put glass back together, when we all know, that's a long shot.

Following the death of my mother, I had a dream: I was standing on the side of the road holding a medium piece of glass in the palm of my left hand. With my right hand, I gathered tiny particles of glass up from the ground to join with the larger piece, in hopes of repairing it.

Glass is not the same once shattered; however, we are forced to rebuild our lives, bit by bit, after death claims the life of someone we loved so dearly.

We must be very careful with grief. If nothing is done to bring some type of hope or relief, depression will quickly take over.

Death proves to us that we ultimately have no control. We can go years and years getting what we want, ordering people around, making plans and managing life according to our fleshy desires, yet when it comes to death, we have no voice or power. That's a reality check that many humans are unable to handle.

Death can cause you to go from being an extrovert to an introvert, overnight!

There are stages in grief that I was clueless about until I was forced to walk through the valley of the shadow of death.

You may experience anger, regret, loneliness, and helplessness. You might even feel as if you're going insane and from what I'm told, all of the above are normal. There were people around who had experienced a loss, so I was wisely counseled.

Even with all of that, I still had days where I didn't want to hear what anyone had to say.

Consider the following:

- Not everyone has the wisdom to advise or comfort you during a time of loss.

- Some people make grief worse by bringing up certain matters, jumping to conclusions and asking to many questions too soon.

- You may not want to be bothered by strangers or even friends during this time; however, company will aid in stimulating your mind.

I will admit, some individuals are not well seasoned on what's appropriate and what should be left unsaid, so I do understand the perspective of not wanting to be bothered. You might even become irritated by those who flaunt what you've lost. In my case it was my mother whom I had to say goodbye to. The last thing that I wanted to see or hear about were mother-daughter activities: cruises, birthday party celebrations, spa dates and photoshoots.

Seeing people with their Mom's right after losing mine filled my throat with vomit!

People will quote scripture and tell you all types of things in attempt to comfort you, but until they have to slip their feet into these cold-hard shoes, their comments and suggestions are bias and sometimes irritating and inconsiderate!

When I originally started this book, I had no idea that I would experience such a monumental loss. There were no clues that I would have to coach myself along with coaching you.

Although the world was moving as normal around me, I was frozen in time. In my grief, I retracted back to the mental state of a little girl, longing for my mother. Some days, in my mind, I was in a dungeon without air, strength, and stripped of the will to nurture myself. There are moments when I blame myself. Sometimes I feel like I let her down, even though, I gave my all. There are moments when I feel like screaming. Sometimes I feel like running full speed, destination unclear.

Nights are better, but I can't forget how strenuous the first few were, following the transition of my mother. I struggled to sleep as I could feel the spirit of torment all around me. Although I consider myself a spiritual warrior, in my travail, my strength was depleted. It's like a demonic team showed up to spiritually mock and sling me around. I've never experienced anything so terrible! **I felt wrong for eating. It felt too much like a celebration. I felt wrong for thinking about advertising. It felt too much like moving forward. I felt wrong for getting dressed. That felt too much like living. I didn't want company. That felt too much like a party. After all, the person who I normally gathered with was gone. I didn't want to laugh. I didn't want to pretend to enjoy hearing people talk about their parents, who were still alive. I certainly Did Not want to hear My Mother being spoken about in past tense. I didn't want to be nice. I wanted answers-relief. I wanted more time with her. I was not ready to be Motherless. I wanted to be SELFISH!**

Death is real and so is **GRIEF**. It will have you all over the place. It will remind you that time ran out. It will assure you that you moved too slow. All that you refused to say will have to forever remain in your heart. All that you were unable to do, even now, in your days of success, you are forever blocked from doing, at least for that person. Grief will fill your mind with regret and heart with sadness.

Now, what about you?

Did you see yourself in one or many of the previous mentioned sentences?

Let's talk about solutions.

1. If you're reading this, that means you're not finished with your earthly assignment. Certainly, you must have a purpose.

2. Make up your mind that you will live and be productive. **This only works if you actually desire to live!** Speak out statements that give you a boost; for example, "This is the day that the Lord has made, I will rejoice and be glad in it".

3. Learn to genuinely celebrate and be happy for those who have what you've lost. The benefits are impressive. There is no justification for envying or treating them ill for having what you miss or desire so much.

My saving grace has been having individuals in my world who don't have pity on me. They discuss things with me that take my mind away from grief and pain. They invite me to partake in activities and conversations that allow me to relax, laugh and inspire myself while inspiring them.

Most of the callers and texters will stop reaching out to you after the first week of saying goodbye to your loved one, but there are a few will remain consistent.

Enjoy these individuals and receive all that they have in their hearts to give. You need them. Believe it or not, they also need you.

4. Take a deep breath and start enjoying the moment. The thoughts of your loved one will always be with you. You are not wrong for taking part of the life that you have been blessed to live. After all, you are alive!

"I have a long road ahead", was my train of thought, until I remembered that my mother was not my possession. Her soul belongs to God, as does mine. My responsibility was to respect, honor and appreciate her while I had the privilege. I did that. She has completed her assignment and entered into a brand-new world. It would be selfish of me to refuse to accept her incredibly awesome new life. Although my heart still hurts, it's a dishonor to desert my earthly assignment by lying in the bed of defeat and depression.

Please understand that there is more to life than crying and wallowing in the land of our losses. We only get so much time to complete our assignments and I strongly discourage the dragging of your feet!

Grief will tell you that you're alone and can't possibly continue on without the person you love, but that's false. One job of the spirit of depression is to assure you that you are nothing without the person who passed away. This is a LIE. Their passing doesn't chain you to a tree unless you allow it.

Moving forward does not mean you have forgotten your loved one. It means, you care enough about yourself to live, free from the bonds of depression.

1.2 No Beau

As with depression, there are levels in loneliness and people will do strange things in attempt to offset the depressive feelings associated with this force.

When you want something and can't seem to have it, the craving for it seems to intensify. For every minute that you go without it, a piece of you seems to get more impatient and even hopeless as your chance to find love appears as a distant wonder. Seeing others in blissful relationships, when you're lonely, can not only sadden you, but welcome the spirit of envy. When your relationship goes down the drain, your emotions can really run wild. Heartbreak has the tendency of tossing people into the sea of loneliness at a rapid rate. The following comments and questions are familiar in terms of heartbreak.

"Why doesn't he want me anymore?"

"Why couldn't she see that I was all about her?"

"What's wrong with me? As soon as I give my heart to someone, they break it."

"Seems like everyone is in a relationship, except me."

Heartbreaks are never easy and it sucks to be in this zone. You want to get out and have fun, but your mind is stuck on your ex. You want to focus on other things, but you seem stuck in the zone of heartbreak.

Being invited to bridal parties, weddings, or any couples-event, can really have you in your feelings. You might even go home to drown in your tears after such occasions.

I know it's difficult being single when all of your friends and loved ones are married; whether or not they're happy is not the principle or concern. You just want someone to love you.

Looking around at others can actually become a problem. Please understand that we are all in different phases and seasons of life. In other words, what does your friend getting married, divorced or engaged have to do with you?

How dare you measure the state of your love life based on what your associates are doing?

Their personal decisions have nothing to do with the rate at which you move, regarding your love life. We must learn how to focus on what's best for our world, according to the season that we're in. Regardless of how blissful others seem, you don't know all of the details surrounding their personal lives and really, it shouldn't be your concern.

One more time: you're not moving too slow, unattractive, or weird for not being in a relationship. It does not diminish your value, so don't beat yourself up for it. Perhaps you have more grounds to cover, more people to assist, more goals to reach as an individual before partnering with someone.

So, shine as an individual.

Reach goals as an individual.

Make an impact on society as an individual and on that particular day when you lock eyes with your love, they'll know that you're suitable for them, because *you stood out as an individual.*

Until that time, you are still worthy to receive love, attention, and validation. You must treat yourself with the highest form of respect and care. With that being said, what are you doing with your life besides grieving the absence of a beau?

I speak about the use of gifts, talents, and skills on a large level, so I must bring attention to that. Beyond occupying your life with the aforementioned, there are many things available to keep you busy.

> **<u>Outside the Home</u>**

1. Volunteer at a shelter, charity, church, or school.
2. Finally execute goals you've put off, which will definitely consume any idle time.
3. Join a support, traveling, or adventure group.
4. Get to know yourself. Spend quality time alone.
5. Mentor someone.
6. Go on scavenger hunts to familiarize yourself with your city of residence and surrounding areas. This is a great way to get out and meet new people.
7. Finally visit and take time with family members that you've been blowing off for months to years.

8. Get involved with events occurring in your city and surrounding areas. Sometimes, nice bonuses float into your world when you're not searching.

9. Join the City Improvement League.

> **<u>Inside the Home</u>**

1. Organize/Clean.

2. Get a pet to care for.

3. Home Improvement Projects.

4. Hobbies that relax the mind.

5. Watch television or web specials that inspire you, make you laugh, or offer hope and solutions.

6. Read, study, and listen to music that makes you feel limitless.

7. Work on and perfect your craft. Revisit old goals.

8. Host intimate parties with drinks and appetizers. Open the floor for relevant topics that your guests can relate to. This is a great tool that reveals how connected and similar

we all are. You will discover that you're not alone in the way that you feel.

There is so much to do and so little time. If you actually have time to sit and torture yourself with thoughts regarding how lonely you are, you could turn those moments into something beneficial. Sometimes when people aren't ready to come out of loneliness, they will assure you that they've done all that there is to do, which is totally false. My father, Anthony Holmes, would often say, "The room for improvement will never be filled." There will always be something more that we can do to enhance our lives or the lives of others. Our work here on Earth is never done, until we're gone. Work, money and assets will not hold you at night, but commitment to your purpose will certainly help you sleep at night. You will be so worn out that there won't be any time for you to sit up and eat ice-cream and cookies.

1.3 Loneliness in Marriage Uncensored.

In order to be someone else's partner, you must be aware and productive in your life as a single person.

Wholeness is necessary before you get with someone. Looking for someone to complete you is not the best idea, as they'll never be able to satisfy that criteria. You may experience the bliss of it all for a period, but eventually, "life" will remind you of your subjection to the many twists and turns that your individual path has set up for you.

People whom have never been married tend to view marriage as the answer to offsetting loneliness. While marriage is a partnership, it is not the answer to all of your dreams nor will it fill all voids. As someone who counsels, you'd be stunned to know the amount of married people who still have lonely nights, although their spouse sleeps next to them!

In a perfect marriage, this should not happen, but *tah-dah*, nothing is perfect.

Some spouses claim not to know how to communicate or initiate anything; however, these same individuals will initiate a new relationship with a stranger and whip out creativity to win them, although their spouse is *lonely* at home. Bare in mind that they are clueless when it comes to their spouse, but full of ideas with strangers.

Marriage requires two worlds to fuse together. Their issues become yours. Times will arise when you will be too frustrated or pissed to go back and forth to clear the air with your mate. If you refuse to exercise self-control and make that unnecessary statement anyway, you just might end up in the quiet zone where days pass without any words being spoken to each other.

This is a lonely place and while I am pro-communication, I have experienced this in my own marriage. People in bliss would probably disagree, but time brings about a change.

- People change.
- The things that brought satisfaction initially, will no longer appease them.
- They may require more or less.
- They could change for better or worse. Stubborn and heartless behavior may become the new norm for a spouse who has

been through hell and high water after experiencing life-altering matters.

- Even the sweet and humble spouses get tired and lonely when their good no longer makes the cut.

When they are constantly abused and taken advantage of, their energy will change toward their overbearing spouse. The same one-in-a-million characteristics that made them a *trophy spouse* will become ancient history, as they have become disgusted with being a *lonely* human waste basket. It's much more to marriage than hugs, kisses, and sex whenever and however you want it.

Your spouse is your best friend, at least they should be. If you have ever had a spouse to be impatient, inattentive, or nonchalant regarding your needs, then you know the loneliness among other things, that this treatment causes.

Three major factors that cause one or both people in a marriage to feel lonely are: inattentiveness, familiarity and lack of understanding.

Inattentive. As a human, you're expected to sleep, but when you handle your spouse as if your eyes are wide shut, that's a problem. Your spouse shouldn't have to cry on someone else's shoulder when they have you. Your spouse shouldn't have to go out in search for relief when you're sitting on the couch watching television.

How can you have a peaceful night of sleep when your spouse is awake and stressed to the max? The same thing that was done to win the hearts of our mates should be the exact routine followed to keep them satisfied.

Tune into your spouse. Open your eyes. Stop taking glances and actually observe them. Ask questions to ensure they're okay. It's your responsibility. You stood before the minister and witnesses to make vows and within those words, you created an expectancy. Do what you promised or get lost.

Why stay in a relationship or marriage when you know you don't care to give the energy that it takes to maintain it?

While I do not condone creeping or slipping out on your mate, inattentiveness is a reason why some make the choice of committing adultery or engaging a side-piece. I mean, everyone wants to be heard, caressed and made to feel alive at some point.

Never become so familiar with your spouse that you don't know when they're bothered, stressed or ready to jump off the Tallahassee bridge! Never allow marital trials to set you on "mute". You know, when you live with each other, but refuse to converse with each other. Instead of dining together, you take your food to a separate room or eat before you get home. You carry on for a day or sometimes longer as if your mate doesn't exist; although they're under the same roof! Being treated in this way definitely causes loneliness. It's hypocritical to celebrate the people at work, compliment other women or men, encourage the orphans, praise the Lord in a church, yet come home with the slightest idea of what your spouse needs.

Oh wait a minute, "everyone knows what their spouse needs", so allow me to restate that. Spouses in this category *don't care or believe it's necessary* to invest the time into getting to the bottom of the issue, because they know that their spouse will eventually "be okay" or "get over it". This is familiarity at its worst!

Misunderstanding. Sometimes we think we KNOW so much when we have the slightest clue. As I stated before, things change and so do people. You may believe your spouse is just "having a moment", but if you actually ask, you'd know that someone has discouraged them, the finances are in default or the kids need a little more help than anticipated.

Just because a man goes off by himself, it doesn't mean that he doesn't want to be bothered with you. Perhaps the pressure on his shoulders have maximized, his demands at work could have increased or maybe he's trying to figure out how he can manage the major demands of life and his entire household without ending up in a hospital. When placing your spouse under the lens of a microscope, it's easy to find the areas where they are in lack; thereby throwing yourself into depression, because you feel ignored. As mentioned above, there are factors that can cause loneliness in marriage, but at other times, understanding is the key. For this reason, study your mate to ensure your awareness of the full scope before you call it loneliness.

Get busy with your individual goals, responsibilities and with pulling your share of the weight. By doing so, you won't have so much time to complain about how lonely you feel.

If an idle mind is the devil's playground, how much damage can he do with loneliness?

Factor 4 Challenge

Loneliness starts as a thought. It causes one to examine their life against others'. If the results show that you are incomplete, single, and clueless to your purpose, you identify yourself as lonely. You may in fact be single, but that doesn't make you eligible to apply for the loneliness group.

Get up and do something about boredom and idleness. Your reality of loneliness is unfathomable to others who see life as a grand opportunity to embark on new endeavors. Getting caught up in the emotions of the moment does not outweigh your possibilities. Get on board with life and the rest will follow. Loneliness is just a film that attempts to blind you from realizing the true essence of time and purpose.

Factor 5

Bullying Exposed

A stigma exists for those who are victims of bullying. It says that something must be awkward about you in order to face the harsh treatment from an oppressor. It says that you are delusional and your claims are outrageous. Let me make this clear right now. You are not the issue. By their actions, bullies prove that they are incapable of managing their issues in a healthy and just fashion.
For whatever reason, they feel as if they need an outlet to display their insecurity, because that's exactly what it is. I am so sorry that you were

selected for their foolish actions, but please don't allow them to drive you over the edge.

People of this caliber are not confident in themselves, only in their ability to abuse their power. They prey on individuals who are, from their tunnel minded view, unguarded and afraid to stand up for themselves. This makes them feel powerful; nevertheless, they are weak squirrels who appear as strong lions. Think about this: if someone is happy with themselves and their reality, why would they allot time to torment others?

Bullying is not limited to people of low privilege, but it exists across the landmarks of religion, politics and nationalities.

1.1 Oppression

Bullying and oppression are best friends, like the interstate and its emergency lane (shoulder road). They go hand in hand. Over the last few years, there has been a tremendous increase in the number of advocates stepping up to create awareness, protection policies, and support groups for those who experience such atrocities; however, discussing *oppression* is like begging for friction.

While most people will agree that bullying children should have major consequences, they will not expect the same for those that bully certain nationalities of people. In many cases, getting the same people to acknowledge that oppression exists would mirror finding a contact lens in a puddle of mud. Ambassadors for anti-oppression are also large in numbers; nevertheless, they are viewed as troublemakers to society.

Their lives are threatened and they are bullied on their jobs. In the case where their voices are heard and others get on the anti-oppression bandwagon, their possessions and reputation may become the sacrifice for their boldness. Anti-oppressors are also among the last considered for promotion, support, or recognition. For this reason, lips are zipped and heads are turned as people aren't necessarily thrilled about suffering the consequence for speaking up.

An oppressor is in fact a bully.

They are synonyms.

They will manipulate those that they deem eligible for their cruelty. They will falsify on information and will transform into the great Samaritan of Jerusalem when placed under the microscope. They have a talent for making themselves look extravagant at the expense of their victims (footstools) being seen in a dark-cast.

1.2 Status Bullies.

When people view others as weaker vessels, they tend to target them for bullying, taking advantage of the chance to feel grand. People in certain positions of authority will use their power to bully and silence the voices of those with ideas for change. An example of the former would be the government having certain laws and policies in place to shut out or dwindle the voices of specific groups of people such as immigrants, minorities, and ex criminals. *This is also a form of social repression.*

> ➤ Bosses bully their employees. They know that certain employees are bound to their jobs, due to their needs, yet they pound on

the pressure; knowing that those individuals will never refute their bizarre treatment.

➤ Husbands bully wives to the point of them being afraid to speak up regarding what they actually desire. They end up submitting to rules and regulations that make their lives a living hell.

➤ Wives bully husbands; especially in terms of finances. They will push their agenda until their husbands are overwhelmed in debt, confusion and discord, which rips away trust and peace within the home.

➤ Siblings bully each other into situations that would otherwise be avoided if they were of no-relation. They will use the blood-factor as means to get what they want.

➤ Neighbors bully each other to the extent of some breaching their lease and pulling out equity earlier than planned, to find solace in a separate area of the city.

➤ Teachers bully students. Although they have their degree, somehow, they have failed at discovering their passionate niche. They make comments like, "I have my degree. You have yours to get." Teachers like this make getting an education feel more like you're being head screwed!

➢ Pastors bully their members. Scriptures and passages are quoted to deceptively influence the hearts of people in believing that God is behind their egotistical desires. This form of manipulative-bullying results in servitude and giving money (from the pot of their needs), because their blessings are supposedly based on their obedience to the Pastor.

➢ Lawmakers bully citizens in the form of written policy that stipulates people from exercising within limits that they would normally have. Oppressive type laws are parallel to the catch 22 dilemma which means, citizens could attempt to live a progressive life, but due to standing laws, they are bound to stagnation.

If you're confident in your position in life, why would you to resort to extreme and unjust measures to protect your spot?

The position belongs to you until it's time for a successor. Humans have a hard time accepting that fact, but it comes along with life. There will be a time when someone else will stand in the very position you currently hold. I guess, to offset the time at which people have to come to terms with that reality, they will conjure up lies, make threats, and exalt themselves to keep their status.

The thing with status is: *one day it will change.* Bullying may slow up the process, but it can't prevent it. Destiny will be.

Bullying is rooted in a dissatisfied spirit that is entertained by taking power over others. When a person has been *bullied or oppressed* for so long, it's like being literally stuck between the same rock and wall of steel. Based on the history of their predictable circumstances, suicide may appear as the best escape. Not only would bullies agree, but you'd be one less person alive that they're threatened by.

1.3 Actions against bullying.

Educate Yourself.

Unless you are in a critical position where the law is against you, you have options. Whatever is being perpetuated over your head is not the final verdict. Other resources exist. Knowledge is not reserved only for a particular class of people. Access is given to those that create it; therefore, create your own opportunity if you have to. Ask questions and research other methods by which you can acquire what you need, without being belittled and classified as incompetent.

There are many ways to get to Nebraska, but from the perspective of one that's 8 minutes away from the state line, it's only one way. It's your responsibility to search out and unlock the information needed for your life. Don't give bullies the satisfaction of feeling like they're your only option. When oppressors know you need them, they will use cunning tactics to ensure your allegiance. Keeping you indebted to them is their mission. If showing up to the funeral of your loved one will create the illusion that they care, they will do it in a heartbeat. Bullies are very much aware of the weaknesses of the submissive, so keep your discerning eyes open.

Dealing with bullying within a marriage requires more careful thought, as it's a critical situation. It is not as simple as reporting an incident to a principal or guidance counselor. Some people, especially wives, are living under quite unfavorable conditions and they feel as if they have no refuge. Their chauvinistic husbands have ostracized them from their families and created enmity so strong that bridges have been burned. In situations like this, there are options where the proper authorities can get you out and into safety. How much longer can you emotionally deal with physical assault? You have become the outlet for him to release his anger. How much more can you bear before you take action against yourself? Antidepressants are of no use in this case. The root of the problem has to be dealt with. Until that's rectified or you remove yourself from the bullying, you will continue to live in fear of his next demonic episode, which could in fact kill you.

1.4 Say Something.

If they're ignoring your opposition of their abuse, report them to higher authority. If it's higher authority, you may just have to escalate it to the corporate level and maybe even beyond. Think of how they make you feel and put an end to their habit of bullying others.

There is a change that's flowing throughout this nation. That change is in the form of speaking up. Many previous bullies are standing on pins as they pray and hope that their victims keep silent. If something is committed against your will, speak up. Don't hoard the pressure. It's not okay for you to constantly live in anxiety.

Tell someone. It's okay to be afraid as long as you report it to someone who isn't. There are trained individuals who know how to deal with bullies. Back when I was in school, you simply got the daylight kicked out of you when you bullied people; especially when you messed with someone's relative.

There was a particular girl that I was bullying, until she could no longer take my crap. When she was finished with me, I had to regain my composure as she had knocked me into the galaxy! I saw stars floating around for a few seconds and had to bear the shame of getting dealt with. Not condoning violence, just saying, everyone will not go home to weep. They will handle you in a way that you won't soon forget. Allowing bullies to have their way with you empowers them, at the expense of shoving you into the grave. Don't destroy your life, due to someone who doesn't understand what it means to live.

1.5 Personal account.

I have personally reported several people who attempted to make my life miserable. As an adult, I have witnessed bullies lose their jobs, possessions, and credibility.

I have seen those of prominence reduced to that of what they previously despised in others. In school, I remember dealing with "comment" bullies, who tried to reduce me by their words. There were mean who found pleasure in bashing any appearance that failed to resemble theirs. Guys slammed me for not having boobs and a big butt like the other girls. Certain teachers bullied me by their assertion of authority. Personal redirection would have done the job, but they were comfortable embarrassing me in the presence of my peers.

Back in elementary, a particular teacher took out approximately 10 minutes to give various explanations for why a student's name was incorrectly spelled and pronounced. With her dry erase marker, she wrote different versions of his name, being sure to flirt with the lines of calling his mother a failure at literacy. Even back then, I thought it was unnecessary and it should have been a conversation for my classmate's mother, not him, and certainly not before the entire class.

That was a day that I felt the weight of bullying and it wasn't me under examination.

This was well over 20 years ago and my classmate has yet to go by his birth name. I would be in utter shock to find out that her diminishing demonstration had nothing to do with it.

That experienced changed me. I knew that I probably hadn't done everything right by my friends and sitting through that episode, seeing his reaction, made me sour towards being the person that fostered shame and pain to others.

I didn't report her. I should have. At that time, I didn't think to. After all, I was a child and she was the adult. I was taught to respect adults and to never challenge authority.

Hmmm, the very reason why many remain silent regarding the abuse and bullying they undergo. Her fiasco, along with being familiar with both sides of the spectrum, served as the root of why I started standing up to bullies, reporting them and advocating for the victims of bullying.

We have to think of those coming after us who will be strained by those who carry on as bullies. Think of how you've carried the pressure of taking no act against bullying. Give someone else the freedom to live without being oppressed, silenced, and damaged by this cringing force.

<u>Factor 5 Challenge</u>

Bullies must be held accountable for their actions. This is made possible when you stand up and speak up. Don't you dare buckle down, telling yourself, "they will stop eventually" as the anxiety builds within you, making it difficult to exercise in your ability to thrive as an individual. You don't need to stay quiet or remove yourself from them. When you *take your life*, they win and continue the cycle of bullying others; especially, if you never spoke up about their harassment. There are regulations and policies that govern bullying. Access those policies and solicit the assistance of those who are competent in enforcing those policies.

Factor 6

Bid the Skunk Farewell

What's that smell?

An extensively popular reason for *purpose suicide* (life stagnation) and disgust is due to the difficult task of moving beyond cringing secrets or instances from yesterday. Certain stories are shared and it gives the notion that some individuals were never loved or conceived with joy and expectancy; nevertheless, they are here.

If you happen to be one who had a rough start in life, you may struggle with how to move forward-knowing you're the product of someone's regret.

One way to cross that bridge is to center your thoughts around making life peaceful and productive for yourself, not those in question. How others who reject you feel, along with their wishes, regrets, and burdens is not your issue.

There was a time when others were responsible for your development, but now you have been released to call the shots, think and act according to the way of your choosing.

So what, they failed you!

So what, they abandoned you!

For whatever reason, they bombed and that was their decision. Now you get to make the choice: live in doom or according to the reason for your existence.

When it comes to reminiscing, happy memories are preferred over the horrific. I mean, who wants to be reminded of anything that fuels anger, grief and abandonment?

No one who wishes to remain in good spirit would be willing to unravel previous chaos, unless they have made peace of some sort with the situation.

Making peace with situations, especially those involving unapologetic people is quite the task. You know, the individuals who are never wrong, who give some off-the-wall excuse for their destructive actions?

Yeah, people of that class are hard to deal with, let alone forgive. Please understand that what was done to you was not okay and you've suffered long enough with questions, that will probably never be answered, to your liking.

Just as someone who was previously in love would seek closure for why their relationship went south, I'd like to suggest that you go back for this exercise. Perhaps you've swept painful matters under the rug for years, but the debris of it is still evident in your daily life. *It's like a personal souvenir.* Regardless of the experience, the connection has to be clipped. Like a florist trimming lifeless pieces from a blooming plant, it's essential for you to do the same. Any memory that inhibits your ability to trust, love or take chances should be deemed powerless, as far as your progress is concerned.

When you continue to wallow in the past, you are feeding it. This is why memories seem to intensify and rarely fade. If you want something to thrive, give it everything pertinent for survival.

In order for something to die, the life supply has to be cut off. Although a bag of potato chips isn't the best option to gain the needed minerals and nutrients, it will remove hunger if enough are consumed. So even at minimum measure, the creeping memories of the past are very much alive. You may not address it, but it sets the tone for the way that you govern your life. Your deep pain may be unknown to those around you; however, it's has a way of rearing its head by the way you manage your life.

The state of denial also acts as a feeding tube. Your way of dealing may be to deny what happened by refusing to discuss or accept it; moreover, the feelings and emotions are as fresh as yesterday when you're triggered to remember.

Many of us have distasteful memories from yesterday, but it's left in the desert where it happened. It doesn't get the satisfaction to linger in our space or interrupt our lives. We grieved back when we parted ways. Perhaps you need to grieve once more, if that will give the needed closure to finally release it.

Some offenders (of various sorts) have gone on to establish careers, marriages and legacies, while their victims struggle to disconnect from the occurrence that changed their life 14 years ago.

Do selfish people sleep well at night or regret the trouble that they've caused?

I don't know.

What I am sure of is my empathy towards any person who has felt pressured to sweep their true feelings under the rug to avoid being roughly examined. I can relate. To any individual who is questioning why they were selected to be abused, then expected to recover by someone else's time frame, you have my empathy. I see you and I don't want you to feel ostracized any longer.

There are so many people who have suffered at the hand of people who were abused themselves, yet they adapted a fresh mentality and broke the curse someway. Others continue to reflect back on the ill treatment that they encountered as a vehicle to receive pity along with a pass. When a person has been evaluated and diagnosed as "crazy", then it has been proven that there is a valid problem that is under continuous professional care. Regular old egomaniacs have no excuse when it comes to emotional and psychological damage that they inflict on the innocent or unexpecting.

My aim is to stand with you while you clip, detach and disconnect from the stain of the occurrence. Sure, the years have passed but when certain memories habitually lead you to drugs, alcohol, or erratic behavior, it proves that you're having trouble recovering without the aid of a substance. "Well, I'm not holding on to it. I just need relief every now and then".

If you discover that your tasteless reasoning behind certain things are directly linked to an episode of mental, physical or emotional abuse, it's a great chance that you're still connected (holding on).

Now, I want to address those of you that have been the offender. Obviously, the state of your mind has changed since you committed the offense, so it's time to set yourself free and live.

Reaching out to the individuals that you pained is also essential to your freedom as well as theirs.

That's called closure and allows for restoration, not to that person per se, but for the state of your own soul.

Refusing to deal or discuss the past isn't a healthy or effective way to separate from it. It simply remains as the skunk in the room that no one can see, but everyone can smell!

That skunk has caused you to self-construct a cement wall that blocks you from experiencing life in its fullness.

Bid the skunk farewell. Trash the souvenir. Open the door to your mind and soul and let it escape.

No, you won't forget, but you can certainly learn how to manage.

Ugly Souvenir

Today I starve the culprit and trash the souvenir,
anything that threatens my peace, I wish not to hear-
No longer will hurt blind me,

no longer will discouragement lead me-

I will not feed negativity, at the expense of my integrity-

I will give myself a chance, to view my possibilities from

an optimistic stance,

Happiness doesn't have to be a fairytale, if I can just

close my eyes and exhale-

If I cease from my wallowing in pain,

perhaps I can change my name-

change my direction, transform my perspective-

Shame will no longer speak for me and Fear must take a

seat-

I will set the tone to survive,

for my soul has been revived-

I have reasons to live,

I must model how to forgive-

The power to overcome darkness is within me,

the wickedness of the past is forever beneath me.

<u>Factor 6 Challenge</u>

If the past contained the power to destroy you in the midst of chaos, that would make this moment a fantasy. Souvenirs are designed to remind you of something beautiful and memorable, so if you have something on the shelf of your heart that represents everything dark, bid it farewell and toss it out.

Factor 7

Rethink Your Existence

First, you must KNOW that you deserve to be here.
Second, you must dismiss any view or opinion
contrary to supporting your right to be here.
Finally, you must take charge of your life like you
BELIEVE you matter!

Contrary to how you may feel, there are reasons
why you're here other than consistently living from
disappointment to heartbreak, to total distress.
Although you didn't select your parents or
purchase a ticket to come to Earth, you were placed
here for reasons that you have yet to discover.
There are several things that can occur in life that

obstructs the power of knowing why you exist. Being too busy, following the trend and wallowing in yesterday's vomit are 3 complexed reasons why people forget or never realize their purpose for being alive.

This is the moment where you must place yourself under the microscope and closely examine your existence, your essence. The terms of negativity have kept you on the brink of breakdown for too long, so trash everything opposed to your being happy. Yes, you can actually BE Happy.

1.1 Goodies

You didn't arrive into this world empty. Something amazing was placed inside of you and guess what, it was perfect! The task is to figure out how to sufficiently make use of that authentic gem, talent or skill that's very much a part of you. It's a great chunk of the reason *why you're here* and when you never discover it or make proper use of it, you may start questioning your reason for sticking around. Though it may seem small, your gift is a large portion of your chemical makeup. If it weren't, you wouldn't be so distraught about being prevented from doing what makes your heart merry.

As mentioned in another read of mine, *"Crazy Enough to Jump"*, "everyone isn't aware of their talents and gifts. Some people discover their 'IT' factors earlier in life. Others search for their identities through a series of jobs, hobbies, and interests until BOOM! They get an epiphany and sometimes in the center of chaos, purpose is uniquely discovered and gifts are unveiled."

So, how are key assets recognized?

Life callings are characterized by experiencing total freedom, success and fulfillment when executing a particular skill, talent or gift. Notice, I didn't say anything about money. When a person exercises within an area of great interest, they aren't geared up due to the pay. They are intrinsically motivated by the joy and satisfaction that the specific role provides to them. Although the cash is destined to flow when operating from passion, they do not operate for compensation alone.

The **trinity of life**, as I call it: *fulfillment, success* and **freedom** coincide together and almost never occur without the others.

How can one be a *success* if they are not *fulfilled*? If a person is free, yet unfulfilled, would they consider themselves as a success?

People complain about many things, but rarely their undisputed talent. Your gift is where it's at. Have you ever been involved with something that gave you an indescribable level of gratification? If you doubt that you can feel that way, you are truly missing out on major reasons to live. Take me for an example; put me in a room with one person or a packed auditorium and I will speak with the same urgency and thrill, because of the pleasure that it gives me. In my experience with speaking, I've had people to frown at me, look at their watch, and even get up and walk out; however, the tiny ounces of negativity aren't enough to kill my passion.

Whatever it is that gives you joy: working with disabled children, interior decorating, matchmaking, traveling as a performer with the circus, or creating authentic wedding centerpieces, do it proudly and wholeheartedly. In the beginning stages of using your gift, you may not be able to afford a 7-day excursion or even an ice-cream cone with the works, but you shouldn't call it quits so soon. Truthfully, your gift may never make you millions, but it will render a satisfaction that money can't give.

There are several phases within developing a gift, talent or skill. **The results of perfecting a talent is worth working for.**

Notice I didn't say, "It's worth waiting for", because if you sit around waiting for things to develop, you and that ancient assumption will starve. *Ideas, dreams and visions are as lifeless as a coffin without an enabled body to facilitate them into reality.*

Why are you depending on your job to bring you lasting happiness when you can't make it through one shift without swearing?

When you constantly wake up feeling stressed about going into work, it may be time for a change. When you live like that, it's only a matter of time before you start feeling hopeless, as if that job is your only option. Regardless of how much pressure management applies on you, the company will be in operation tomorrow, *whether you're there or not.* An income must be generated in order to support lifestyles, but more prominence tends to go towards what pays the bills and less towards what truly satisfies you.

When you can't find satisfaction, it's natural to resort to depression as the inner core of you is unfruitful. It's one thing to be dissatisfied along with working behind the scenes to improve your status, but how many people take that chance? Some will remain in positions that they despise because it supports their cravings, not fully realizing that it's the main culprit of their stress. That alone can drive people insane or it can push them to advertise their personal brand. Branding oneself may be a truckload of work, but it should never brew misery and depression.

I'm sure you're thinking, "Why would a successful person be in search for a change in employment or anything else attached to the quality of life?" It's for the very reason that you're seeking a change;

unfulfillment. Fulfillment does not mean that everything will be perfect. Again, for the people in the balcony, *everything will not be perfect,* even in the state of fulfillment. Please don't allow the lack of perfection to lead you away from what you need to Live. For some reason, people assume that wealth with an ideal career equals happiness, but it doesn't. Do you watch celebrity news?

Never experiencing contentment can really drive people over the edge. Operating in areas of sentiment are extremely powerful and keep many alive and peaceful, even though they experience mishaps, loss and pain. There is something soulfully binding about knowing who you are and *why you're here.* Knowing is powerful on its own, but when you live like you're a needed asset to whatever you're associated with, you have a good shot at combating depression and suicide.

1.2 Do What Makes You Happy

While the statement, *"Do what makes you happy"* sounds conclusive, there are some inconsistencies within that cliché that must be clarified; lest you face the unexpected and give up. An example of this would be getting married for the sake of alleged daily *happiness,* totally unaware of the upcoming trials that accompany living as one unit. Almost everything that can be done comes with some type of attachment, so don't bank on receiving a daily dose of whip cream and strawberries.

Below is a list with items that "make people happy" against reactions that may occur. The following graph is just an example of some things that trickle along with doing "what makes one happy".

What Makes You Happy	*Possible Unforeseen Occurrences*
Showing your love through purchasing gifts	A lack of interest in the gifts.
Entertaining or Hosting Events	Robbed or Blackmailed by guests.
Caring for children	Falsely accused of being an unfit caregiver.
Being a teacher	Exposed to troubled students and families.
Family Mediator	Excommunicated for allegedly having bias views and favoritism.
Being a surgeon	Clarifying high risks against low advantages.
Opening Dream Company	Insufficient earnings for personal and professional use.

People are often discouraged from the very things that make them happy because they assume that their problems will end. If the bumps in the road aren't enough to throw them off course, then it's the false belief that being in an ideal situation is free from disappointment.

Doing what makes you happy gives you a reason to get out of bed, anxious about the day ahead.

Participating with the things that gives you joy is one of the most beneficial moves that one can make. Sure, you may have to work hard at it, lose sleep and friends, but the satisfaction that it renders gives you the fuel required for living a purpose filled life.

One day Tangy, an associate of mine was complaining to Patty, a mutual associate of ours, about a certain woman who was resistant to her ideas. Every time she attempted to move on a plan, this woman would react with sarcasm and rejection. Patty listened to Tangy's rant until she raised a single hand and firmly said, "Chew the meat and spit out the bones".
I guess it made since to Tangy as she made no further comments. I certainly locked in the statement and this is what I gathered. Everyone will not be excited for you or happy to have your around. Some will actually hate your guts, but their misery is powerless when weighed against your passion to do *what you love*. That's what it is my friend, misery. If they were so comfortable and satisfied with their choices and status in life, they wouldn't exude so much negativity. Forget their criticism and focus on mastering your craft.

1.3 Purposely Involved.

A good way to keep oneself in the safe zone is to get purposefully involved with auxiliaries that pull from those areas of expertise and passion. One unspoken key with any vocation is, *unfavorable issues will occur*. Trouble, irritation and mistakes are not a sign that you should resign or cease from operating. *You are here* to make your mark and sometimes that mark may get smeared, but it can never be erased.

No matter how many times you're considered irrelevant or unnecessary to a project, please note that you matter and haven't done anything wrong. Perhaps your expertise makes you a threat and now they want to discredit your work.

Unfortunately, you serve alongside those who fear losing recognition, credibility or their status to you. Don't beg and plea for others to appreciate your value when they are adamant about your being elsewhere. If anything, you're better off when people say your service is no longer needed. Leave. Start your own or go where you can shine.

Why linger where you're unwelcomed?

You don't lose value because you let go and move on. You devalue yourself when you stay against your own will and suffer the consequences of holding on. Worth is increased by facing reality and making decisions that improve your situation, whether it feels good or not. Changes hurt and processes will make a warrior out of you.

Let's view the role of a chef for this example. Making the mistake of over-cooking a dish doesn't mean he or she is the worst cook on the planet. One sampler of the food may think it's an incredible dish while another may think the prepared dish is under-seasoned and disgusting.

Is that reason to bash the chef? No way.

If you've ever hosted or been a guest at an event, you can note that a variety of goodies are served in attempt to satisfy the guests.

Ever wondered why?

It has a lot to do with the fact that everyone isn't into the same choices of food and drink items.

My question to you is, why would you store your passion in the attic because a few people had a complaint?

In every vocation, there will be some type of slip-up. Everyone will not produce 100% daily. Mishaps are bound to happen and when they do, reassess and do better next time.

Oh geez, you mispronounced a word during your presentation. Keep going and finish strong.

Whoops, you burned up your signature dish that your guest were dying to taste?

Clearly, if your dish is well-known, your guest will know that it was a mistake. Don't beat yourself up over burned food. Order some take-out and continue in entertaining your guest. As for the cooking slip-up, schedule another date for your guest to try the dish and add in a bonus dessert. Okay, your celebrity client had a wardrobe malfunction? Arrange a complimentary blazing hot photo shoot with the same client to promote their next appearance. No matter how skilled you are, your performance or attempt will sometimes lack perfection. Please remember this when something doesn't turn out as meticulous as you planned. *Don't allow your slip-up to be your funeral.* The following statement is a blunt declaration to your own right to be free to make mistakes. If people don't like what you have to offer, they have the option to seek out what they desire elsewhere. In other words: "If they don't like it, they can leave". Wallowing in a mistake or flop will only worsen the way you feel about yourself. Critiques will run your incident into the ground in attempt to make you look like an amateur, but their evil intent can't destroy your image unless you authorize it. Even if people are discussing your *'moment of shame'* 20 years from now, you'll be able to look at your continuous alcaldes as proof that you kept moving. **Never deny yourself the chance to continue your resume.**

We have to learn to allow fairy tales to be exactly what they are; LIES. That would have blown over a bit easier had I said *fabrication,* which further proves that we have been consuming infant formula far too long. As the days past, we must mature and accept our reality. If it's unacceptable, make the revisions that are within your ability. Freedom, wealth, wisdom and education are all factors that can indeed make life smoother; however, neither of them will eliminate having to stop for a bowel movement.

Yes, I said it. As a human, you will still have to deal with the foul and dirty portions of the human experience.

No one is exempt. So, prepare yourself to effectively deal with the positive and negative, incredibly sweet aromas to the downright funky.

The sooner you learn to refuel and reboot following disappointment, the better you'll be able to manage life. There will be disappointments and even losses along the journey of doing what you love, but resorting to pity and depression will only lock you out of your own destiny.

1.4 Getting Happy Again

One of the most disturbing things that I have heard is, "I don't know what makes me happy" or

"Nothing in my life right now is making me happy."

At some point, you must detach from all duties to:

taste something incredibly delicious,

view something splendid,

touch something authentic,

hear something stimulating,

smell something that takes your mind to paradise,

and imagine something that awakens hope.

If you're clueless regarding how to get the above in motion, start with a few magazines, which are free at your local library.

Don't be so picky about which magazines you take, as you could use some new information. Inside you may find some interest sparkers and attention grabbers. A travel magazine may introduce you to sights you never knew existed. It may spring up the desire to travel, which maximizes your ability to meet others and even discover more about yourself. You'd be surprised by what you can uncover from places you wouldn't normally visit, or from those individuals you would normally ignore. Certain visuals from the magazines may in fact relax your mind and usher you into serenity.

A separate option is to play genres of music that you normally wouldn't listen to. Other tones and tunes used to express meaning and appreciation for life could actually aid in lifting you out of the mental zone of pity. Stop playing the songs that remind you of your ex or anything else that's ancient. Such things keep you buried under the sand.

Get out there and make new memories with new music, new visuals and new associates.

There is so much more to life than the neighborhood you were raised in and the traditions you refuse to break.

Leave your house and get in sync with life.

Add some new titles, places, and experiences under your belt.

Go sign up for a dance, aerobics, or painting class.

Join a committee and finally make use of that degree you worked so hard for.

So what you're in debt? Sitting around stressing about money you don't have is a sure way to age your body and cause your heart to ache. Sure, we are all human and subject to worrying, but we all must ask ourselves,

"How will worrying change my situation?"

While it will not change your status, it will certainly alter your health!

We can worry about the problem or work on a solution.

The difference between the two is, one is beneficial while *the other has the potential to become fatal.*

<u>Factor 7 Challenge</u>

In rethinking your existence, remember that there is always something that you can do. The most difficult part is getting started. I urge and beg you to get started NOW. No more putting it off. No more excuses.

As soon as the urgency rises to change, get up right then and take action. If you stall in any way, there is not much hope for anything changing in your favor.

Do you want to be happy or not?

Your actions will answer that question. You are just as worthy of happiness as anyone else, so get out there and BE.

Factor 8

Those that Matter

Hurricanes and tornadoes are known to rip through cities; leaving shambles behind for relief teams. Life can toss you around just like a hurricane, leaving you feeling like you're better off dead. Every time you attempt to get up, you get another slap upside your head; knocking you to the ground again. As much as you would like to rid yourself of the burdensome feelings, remember that someone is counting on you; especially if you're a parent. Before giving up, consider the folks in your life who actually care for you. Remember those who adore you beyond your flaws. Take note of those who are simply satisfied with your presence alone; those who aren't in constant expectation of what you can do for them.

Think about those who understand your worth and appreciate your impact on their lives. People in this category will be the ones who suffer the cost of your negligence, withdrawal, or absence.

Please omit children from this portion, because they certainly have needs and expectations, as they should. They are innocent, oblivious to danger and in need of guidance.

When the folks that they count on let them down, where can they turn?

When the vacuum of life shows up to suction them through the cracks, you will want to be confident in knowing you did your absolute best by them. You will want to know that they will be able to successfully operate in life, supervised or not.

Doing your best is not defined as doing enough to get the job done or until the person in need shuts-up.

Giving your all is defined as going beyond the request to ensure that all areas are covered.

It's about showing up to give 100% when you're physically exhausted.

Giving your best is about maintaining your integrity in the absence of an observer.

Although you arrived to Earth alone, unless you're a twin or multiple, your decisions are not just about you.

To all parents: Think about what you're up against on a daily basis. How do you think your children, based on their current level of intellect, would handle the same pressure?

Death is certainly part of the human experience; nonetheless, have you given your children the essentials to navigate through life?

Consider the times during your personal journey when you were abandoned, although you were sure that someone would come to your rescue. Knowing this, who do you imagine covering your parental responsibilities, in your absence? Really think about that.

Many will make claims of what they'll do if the time presented itself; however, consider the amount of assistance you currently receive.

Don't put too much trust in areas where it hasn't been proven. One day your descendants will have to step out independently. Until then, do all that you can to prevent them from rising to adulthood prematurely.

The thought of your babies having to manage in this cold world without the proper nourishment, protection and guidance is scary. It should be a thought powerful enough to condition your mind to fight for your peace, especially for the sake of them.

Staying alive just for the sake of being around is about the same as being dead, because you have decided to mentally *check out, creating a barrier between you and those who care.* When depression takes over a person, it's obvious that there is some type of wall blocking their ability to truly live in the moment, embark on new adventures, and make fresh memories.

Attempting to hide depression is of no use, as it's evident during times when you think no one is watching.

Mental and emotional barricades are proven to substantially damage relationships, yet attempts are made to cover or ignore this issue. These barriers are darn near impossible to hide. They are as obvious as a chain locked gate. No key, no entrance. People are very much aware of their loved ones existing in a dark-hole, but they can only do and say so much. The depressed individual has to desire sunlight more than darkness. They must eagerly want to break out of pity and into celebration.
If you're going to live, put it all on the line and live. Putting it all on the line means, you will not allow anything to outshine present moments. It means you will make every attempt to stop seeing the bad in everything.

So much time is spent wondering why certain things happened, whether you would have been further in life, or even if you could've done something to avoid previous disasters. Those answers are as uncertain as knowing the direction of the wind, at any given time.
Your mind must be exhausted from all of the stressful pressure that you're adding to it. Until you

liberate your mind from the chaos, fears, and confusion, it will forever flood your brain. The desire to rest will be present, but with the mind frozen in worry-zone, fully relaxing will be quite the task. You may even wake up totally exhausted as if you never went to sleep. Added pressure and stress will prevent the mind from rebooting as it should while in rest mode. Taunting yourself with the "what ifs" is not only a bad idea, but a terrible one that will more than likely go unresolved. You will never have the answers to certain questions. This present moment is what you have a vote in. Make it count.

Lashing out on children or anyone innocent of committing an offense proves that you dishonor those who care. Don't make the undeserved suffer the penalty for your troubles or losses. They are not responsible for your feelings or the way you view yourself. Give them the chance to enjoy you without the residue of previous frustrations, which stems from separate sources.

Factor 8 Challenge

Before a decision is made to do anything that will negatively alter the lives of those who are counting on you, think of them as cheerleaders. They will root for you even when you aren't doing so well. They will sing your praises when everyone else is in doubt. If you get tackled, they don't stand back and laugh. If your efforts are intercepted, they don't pack up and go home, they shout louder and tell you to *keep going-it's not over*.

They show up, regardless of the nature of the weather to girdle you.

If you leave the field, it's a slap in the face for them. If you quit, their support is in vain. ***Those that matter*** will remind you that winning is possible and a healthy mind is the victory!

Factor 9

RESIDUE on the Filter

Ever wondered why you still feel a bit awkward and bound, even though you've done everything that you thought was necessary to lift your head above water? **Consider the residue on the filter.** Residue is any particle or material that lingers after the original particle has been removed.

Residue is that creepy invisible force that rises within you regarding an issue that you buried a long time ago, or so you thought. Excess will hide out in areas of your intellect, which has the potential to pollute anything good that you have going on.

Mistakes cause residue that some are forced to deal with for the rest of their lives. For this reason, ask questions and never shy away from gaining knowledge out of fearing how others will view you. You will have to live with the residue of your decisions, not those standing back with a magnifying glass.

Just because you've cried, finally revealed your hurt, or got revenge, it doesn't guarantee a clean subconscious. You might even feel worse as doing a little polishing isn't quite enough to land you back to healthy rationing.

This is the part when you have to check the vents, fans, and crevices of your life for remnants left behind. Just as dust can cultivate dust mites, which will in turn cause some to have mild to severe allergic reactions, contaminated residue from the human experience will be a harvest ground for depression and suicidal contemplations.

To spike learning angles, I will describe 'Residue' and its effect on people from the aspect of cleaning styles.

Sanitation is like cleaning your nose on a tissue, disposing the tissue, then washing your hands. It's a system by which all dirty items are removed from an area where human health can be threatened. Bodily waste, expired food, and dead organisms can all be detrimental to the health of a human; especially when it's within a vicinity where most of their time is spent. Taking out the trash gets rid of the bulk of used and toxic items, but it does nothing for the particles at the bottom of the trash bin, that somehow seeped through the bag. The drain in the bathtub will remove the dirty water, but it will not clear the nasty ring from around the tub.

I have yet to observe a city worker clean the dumpster after ridding its elements into the loading portion of the dump truck. The area around a dumpster reeks worse than a gas stations' restroom that hasn't been cleaned in 2 weeks! City workers are very much aware of this, but it is beyond their job description to scrub dumpsters.

Is it safe to say that although the trash was dumped, the dumpster is still an unclean item?

1. **How does this analogy relate to sanitation of the mind and the release of depression?**

Going through emotions; for example, crying about the way you were treated is a form of sanitation. Tears may symbolize the flushing out of your feelings, but the resulting pain and insecurity that was sprouted remains intact. Crying is said to be an act of cleansing the soul and while I won't deny the cliché, cleansing must go further than tears. Tears are a start, but when they never stop flowing over a period of time, a more intense form of help is needed. You are not a wimp for crying, by all means let it out; however, if the grief seems unbearable at times, please make it known to someone who can aid you in managing. Everyone will have to bear situations that are less than perfect at some point and it's nothing worse than acting like you're okay when *you know* you're dying inside.

Disinfecting is the term for going crazy with the antibacterial sprays when you're attempting to keep down germs from areas of your home. If one of your children becomes ill, a pediatrician will urge you to disinfect all surfaces in your home to avoid the potential spread of the germs. Disinfecting involves the cleaning of non-living objects with antimicrobial chemicals, in order to destroy microorganisms that thrive on the surface of non-living objects. Bacterial spores will laugh and consume a bag of popcorn during the disinfection process, because it's resistant to it.

Yes, disinfectants are made with antimicrobial agents, but not the strongest combination of agents. The disinfection process is limited. *Killing all living organisms is well beyond the reach of disinfecting.*

2. **How does disinfection relate to mind sanity and the release of depression?**

Changing your telephone number, burning clothes, relocating, promptly jumping into new relationships, binging on various diet plans, exercising yourself to death at the gym, drastic changes to your hair, picking up habits with conventional soothers, promiscuity, seeking potentially dangerous attention or pretending that it will all vanish if you deny reality, are all forms of attempting to disinfect the mind.

Just as bacteria spores can totally live through a disinfection process, depression will knock on the door of your mind when you finish going through any or all of the motions as listed above. Again, there are areas that are beyond the limits of disinfecting; for example, if resent resides in your heart toward someone, totally avoiding them would be a way of managing (disinfecting-removing yourself from the source of the problem); nonetheless, if you are ever faced with that individual, you can bet your bottom dollar that those feelings of anger and distaste will flare up. *You have not eliminated the problem* nor do you view it differently. All you did, in this case, was spray a disinfectant that is obviously insufficient with handling this type of circumstance.

- Changing your telephone number will not change the fact that your ex took advantage of you.
- Burning clothes will not send the memories of abuse up in smoke.
- Drinking and smoking may take you away for a while, but when its effect wears off, you're still left with a toilet full of...you know!
- Excessive exercising to get the validation you never received is still not guaranteed to happen.

Remember, it's all in your mind. How you feel and the trash left behind is an illusion of your delusional mind, in the opinion of your offender. Trespassers have no idea as to how you feel, so sacrificing your time and effort in attempt to capture their attention is not in your best interest. The aforementioned list is only a few ways that are selected as means of coping, but wouldn't you prefer to have your mind at ease, as opposed to further applying pressure by means of suppression?

Sure, you would and **sterilization** of the mind is the vehicle with the capabilities of destroying the power of purpose-suicide, depression, suppression or total misery! **Sterilization** is the highest and most efficient form of cleaning. It will kill All living microorganisms along with eradicating all particles of **residue**. Sterilization puts on the pressure, turns up the heat, and whips out all of the most robust chemicals to get the job done without leaving any signs that something was present beforehand.

3. **So, what does this sterilization mean for the mind?**

Since the mind is not an object that can be tossed on a surface and sterilized, a different form of sterilization can be taken. As mentioned previously, the brain is a storing facility that archives and recalls information that was formerly processed. While humans are unable to permanently expunge the memories from the brain (with the exception of disruptive accidents), they can learn how to **accept, adapt, and advance.** I call it **AAA** *for the mental operating system.* This means that serious measures are taken to enhance the quality of life as far as pondering is concerned. Remember, the mind is where reasoning, decisions, and imaginations are generated, so if it lingers mostly on unfavorable thoughts, the characteristics of the person will take a turn for the worse. It's impossible for a conceited individual to radiate the lowest measure of confidence in the presence of others. That would contradict the beliefs of their intelligence.

- If you believe you're the scum of the Earth, you will not require much from people.
- If you think your chance for success is blown, you have already counted your losses.
- When you can't satisfy yourself, no career, hobby, or person will have a shot at it.
- When you wallow in your feelings, you accept that nothing is more important.
- If you believe you will never find love, you're partially correct. *Someone will love you, but you won't be convinced.*

Sterilization for the mind involves preparing the mind for transformation. This is the level where excuses are prohibited, because the mind is ready to be unchained.

This is the part where enough becomes enough. You literally decide not to live another day in the dumps. You refuse to sit back and watch everyone else live while you remain idle, voiceless and perfunctory regarding your state of mind, life, and purpose.

You stay on top of your progress by any means necessary. You become unconcerned about your critics and focused on mental freedom.

You clean up your circle and dismiss yourself from any person or group that's anti-productive. You stick to your guns. You don't allow anyone back in your space who comes to remind you of the days of previous misery.

If someone can't love you past your flaws and assist you with discovering solutions, get rid of them. They are residue.

If they think you were more fun when you were depressed, get rid of them. They are residue.

If they prefer to live in the past, get rid of them. They are residue.

"Well, how do you get rid of someone?"

You become unavailable to them. You stop being so easily accessible for them. Avoid answering the phone when they call, because you are already aware of their predictability. Don't go for it. When people change, you will be able to see it, without them going overboard to convince you. If you have to be alone for a season, so be it. Everything that you can see is temporary. You may be in a transition today, but tomorrow will come and you will have the same report of healing as I, along with a countless number of others who have overcome the stain of depression and all particles of residue. It is urgent to surround yourself with an army of positive support. If your support system is unlike anything you've ever tried and it's helping you, stick with it. Sometimes change will totally transform your world, opening you up to new networks and chances that you never imagined. You deserve to wake up with excitement, even on a Monday morning. Ask me how I can be so sure (wink, wink).

<u>Factor 9 Challenge</u>

Analyze your life and search for any hidden residue that makes its peak through your secret thoughts, actions, or choices. If red wine is spilled on a white evening gown, it will cause much stress. Think of residue in this way. In reality, the dress can be taken to a dry cleaner, but certain residue hidden in your brain can destroy your will to live. The day has arrived for you to exterminate any sign of residue that blocks your privilege to smell the coffee and enjoy the breeze.

Factor 10

Invisible Influences on the Mind

There are many beliefs out there and while this section is not meant to discredit any of them, humans are spiritual beings. No spirit, no life. There is an enemy of your soul that you may never see, but the influences are continuous, subtle and cunning.

Ever been in a really good mental space, then all of a sudden, you're feeling irritable. If you're not careful, you will go along with that "mood swing" that has no real basis for influencing you.

Nothing bad happened.

No rain ruined your parade, just a weird, yet strong urge to mentally alter. That's a spirit and its best work is coordinated within the mind. If you tell your doctor about these periodic nudges, he or she will prescribe you something to suppress or alter the "mood swing".

You're probably going crazy with the 'what-about' thoughts like, menstrual and menopausal cases, which are associated with chemical changes and imbalances within the body. Cases such as this are chemical, not spiritual.

If you're familiar with the term *mood*, **it's a synonym to** *spirit*. When someone is hospitable, selfless, and friendly, they are known as "sweet-spirited". A foul mouth along with nonchalant behavior would hintingly describe someone who's in a "bad mood".

If nothing is ever done to get rid of the lingering spirit of sadness, loneliness, defeat, or insecurity, it will become a stronghold (stubborn force that grows on you), which weighs heavily on personality and character.

Antidepressants, alcohol, and conventional soothers are no match for the dispirited. Something stronger is needed. The root has to be nursed. The root is the culprit of the experience, incident or occurrence. The root is often impacted by a seducing spirit that presented itself in times past, but was never rejected. Over time, regular thoughts begin to alter to the extent of you not recognizing the person you've become.

Spirits are similar to people. They hang out with their equivalents. Snakes slither around with snakes and share the habitat with other reptiles. They do the things that are pertaining to a snake like sneak up on their prey, strangle them, then feast. They will not be seen with Eagles. Investors associate with investors and other members of that class. They make decisions that stimulate the economy. You will not see them making plans with fast food cashiers. Spirits are no different. They have buddies.

A spirit of sadness will be accompanied by its associates of loneliness, procrastination, jealousy, low self-esteem, and vulnerability, to name a few.

An example of this would be an *oppressed* wife dealing with feelings of fear, anxiety, and insufficiency.

The purpose of the enemy is to set up illusions to make people doubt the existence and validity of God. The **Enemy (anything or person opposed to you fulfilling the true God-ordained purpose for your life)** of your soul has a 1-3-part mission.

The thief cometh not, but for to steal, and to kill, and to destroy: I am come that they might have life, and that they might have it more abundantly. John 10:10

Translation:

If forces of evil can taint your mind, due to someone or something of great essence being stripped from you, then your thoughts are susceptible to being altered in a negative direction.

STEAL. During a time when you're unaware, something is stolen from you. The thing that will be stolen from you is strategically orchestrated. It's based off what you consider as invaluable. Forces of evil are observant.

They are very much aware of the things you hate and the items or people you idolize. This information is revealed to them by your lifestyle and the subjects you openly discuss. Matters with no significance will rarely spoil your milk, but your pet-peeves and fears will.

Being served divorce papers when you were doing all you could to save your marriage is more so along the lines of what I'm talking about. Finding out that your best friend blackmailed you would take your breath away.

Getting terminated when you had plans to move up in a company, is definitely a slap in the face. Occurrences such as these will internally **ROB** a person of so much. They will feel as if they've been stripped naked! This does quite the number on the brain and becomes the nesting ground for lowly and vengeful imaginations.

<u>KILL.</u> This happens when something ceases to exist. It could be your dreams, goals, or will. An example of this would be hearing the answer "NO" repeatedly, even though you're working hard and persistent for a "Yes".

It's like someone making you a promise, then leaving you out there in expectation, without a word of their negation. It's like being prepared to go back to school, but after handling all of your duties, kids, along with their individual matters, you have no energy or desire to excel. The Mom might even feel guilty for trying to do something to improve herself.

The desire to keep pushing is *killed*, because it's just too strenuous to try.

<u>DESTROY.</u> This one is harsh and will come on you like a wave. It will leave your eyes bulged and jaw on the ground. In this category, the enemy might appear innocently, then go in for the kill. Abuse and deception of all forms are ways that the enemy banks on destroying a person's will to thrive. Backstabbing, harsh criticism, gossip, lies, abandonment, destitution, and an untimely death of a loved one; especially an unjust death, all have heavy influences on mentally destroying people. In many of these cases, individuals don't recover. They are slow to admitting that help is needed, nor do they seek deliverance from the demons that tweak and pervert their minds. This is **destructive.** The enemy is victorious whenever he can check another human being off of his hit list. You don't have to be non-existent in the Earth realm to be dead. Whenever you have lost the will to care for yourself and others, you are a dead person walking!

<u>THE GOOD NEWS</u>

Since you have been unsuccessful in your tactics, I suggest you move toward something stronger and solid. You need something supernatural and permanent. You need something that's everlasting, lifting you up without sending you back down for a crash landing!

It seems like the very mentioning of the Creator gets people into a knot. Many feel judged or sour about discussing God for several reasons. One of the popular reasons is because they have been squandered over by someone who claimed to be a Christian. They have seen behaviors and heard statements that were far from Christ-like.

I want you to erase the negative connotation that has been penciled into your mind about God! Humans can talk about God all day, but they are Not God and will never be His only way to speak to you.

Only HE knows the inner workings of you. He knows our honest feelings, beyond the facades. This is not about judgment, but about a proven, credible, and sustaining form of healing for your mind.

What's so wrong with giving God a shot to transform your life; your mind?

HE is your Creator and knows how to make repairs to his creations.

Seems like people sprint towards temporary fixes while totally rejecting things that can actually help.

Come unto me, all ye that labour and are heavy laden, and I will give you rest. Matthew 11:28 KJV of the Bible.
The above scripture has everything to do with you Surrendering and Releasing.

I did not say that you will forget everything; however, the spirit of love and truth will teach you how to move into psygression, as I uniquely defined back in the section of Factor 1. It's not always about forgetting. The key is to rise above the debris, although you still remember the storm!

You are NOT what happened to you 16 years ago or even 6 months ago. Often, people walk around as if they've committed or undergone the unforgivable. They deem themselves as 'broken beyond repair', so to them, it's a lost cause; however,

"Therefore, if anyone is in Christ, that person is a new creation. The old has gone, the new is here!" 2 Corinthians 5:17 NIV from the Holy Bible.

This reiterates that the old things are unable to stain you. The dirty things of the past do not ruin your shot at experiencing a personal relationship with God. Two people in a thriving relationship will share the same mission, interests, and beliefs.

It's impossible to continually encounter God and keep a mind of turmoil.

The old and stressed mind would be restored. It comes along with the relationship! There is only one condition. You have to genuinely ask HIM to help you. HE has never been into bombarding his way into anyone's life. HE desires to be welcomed. At the feet of Christ is the perfect place to leave the mental weight that has imprisoned you. These weights have served you no benefit.

They have not made you stronger. They have shoved you into an isolated place, where you're unavailable for peace, friendship, and love. These weights are killing you, one day at a time! Let them go. It has to be quite miserable to live behind barricades all the time. Drop them off with the proper authority, so that you can experience the rest and peace you so desperately need.

<u>Factor Challenge</u>

In the midst of you dealing directly with God, there are ministers and mentors who will sit with you just like a therapist, offering support, therapy, and tips for your mental state. *Some ministers are actually certified mental health professionals.* **That may be surprising, but there is a battle for your brain and these individuals understand that some situations have to be handled from diverse angles.**

Strength through Scriptures

The following section is for those of you who can appreciate a spiritual nudge of assistance, especially during those complicated, aggravating, dark, lonely and dry tunneled phases in life.

There is nothing judgmental about the following passages.

If you're willing to give them a chance, I believe that the total belief of these passages can have a profound positive impact on your life and understanding.

+ Can any one of you by worrying add a single hour to your life Matthew 6:27 (NIV)

+ Do not be anxious about anything, but in every situation, by prayer and petition, with thanksgiving, present your requests to God. Philippians 4:6 (NIV)

+ And the peace of God, which transcends all understanding, will guard your hearts and your minds in Christ Jesus. Philippians 4:7 (NIV)

+ Though you have made me see troubles, many and bitter, you will restore my life again; from the depths of the earth you will again bring me up. You will increase my honor and comfort me once more. I will praise you with the harp for your faithfulness, my God; I will sing praise to you with the lyre, Holy One of Israel. Psalms 71:20-22

+ I sought the LORD, and he answered me; he delivered me from all my fears. Psalms 34:4 (NIV)

+ Cast all your anxiety on him because he cares for you. 1 Peter 5:7 (NIV)

+ So do not fear, for I am with you; do not be dismayed, for I am your God. I will strengthen you and help you; I will uphold you with my righteous right hand. Isaiah 41:10 (NIV)

+ For the Spirit God gave us does not make us timid, but gives us power, love and self-discipline. 2 Timothy 1:7 (NIV)

+ Even though I walk through the valley of the shadow of death, I will fear no evil, for you are with me; your rod and your staff, they comfort me. Psalms 23:4 (NIV)

+ "Therefore I tell you, do not worry about your life, what you will eat or drink; or about your body, what you will wear. Is not life more than food, and the body more than clothes? Look at the birds of the air; they do not sow or reap or store away in barns, and yet your heavenly Father feeds them. Are you not much more valuable than they? Can any one of you by worrying add a single hour to your life? "And why do you worry about clothes? See how the flowers of the field grow. They do not labor or spin. Yet I tell you that not even Solomon in all his splendor was dressed like one of these. If that is how God clothes the grass of the field, which is here today and tomorrow is thrown into the fire, will he not much more clothe you—you of little faith? So do not worry, saying, 'What shall we eat?' or 'What shall we drink?' or 'What shall we wear?' For the pagans run after all these things, and your heavenly Father knows that you need them. But seek first his kingdom and his righteousness, and all these things will be given to you as well. Therefore do not worry about tomorrow, for tomorrow will worry about itself. Each day has enough trouble of its own. Matthew 6:25-34 (NIV)

Final Thought

The will of a human is powerful, yet their state of being is based on the direction of their will. A will to live with a stench of doubt could pervert that will. Since actions are based off thoughts, it's urgent for the mind to be strong and healthy.

If you wish not to be governed by a spirit of depression, you have the power to ward it off. Retain and exercise your responsibility to protect your temple.

In **whatever form** that you choose to alleviate depression, please note that any measure will eventually fail if you refuse to transform your thought process.

You can try to force someone to eat, but when they have no appetite, you are in for a fight. Attempting to convince someone of something that their mind is already against is a tiresome battle.

Same principle applies to the state of your mind, which directly influences your decisions. If you aren't willing to accept and work along with the recommendation for your wellness, then that particular plan is in for a fight, *against you*.

About the Author

Antoinette is a bright-eyed woman who views the world from the perspective of many colors. Like an Eagle, she perceives the matters of life beyond the surface level, and is immensely inspired by this gift. Because of her love for people, ministry and coaching is dear to her heart. Among being married to her visionary husband, she's the active mother of their 4 children. Outside of training and innovating, she is entertained by the free things in life, which are best.

Antoinette is also the author of *"Crazy Enough to Jump"*.

To connect with the author, visit www.myaet.net where you will find more links to see and hear her in action. Fan mail is always appreciated. Please forward to info@myaet.net

Other Works
CRAZY Enough To JUMP

"You're Either Leaping in Life or Lounging in Fear."

Available Online. For Signed Copies, visit

www.myaet.net

www.ingramcontent.com/pod-product-compliance
Lightning Source LLC
Chambersburg PA
CBHW061802250726

48657CB00001B/242